Damaged Souls

Damaged Souls

By

GAMALIEL BRADFORD

KENNIKAT PRESS/PORT WASHINGTON, N. Y.

DAMAGED SOULS

Copyright 1923 by Gamaliel Bradford
Reissued in 1969 by Kennikat Press by arrangement
with Houghton Mifflin Company
Library of Congress Catalog Card No: 77-85990
SBN 8046-0541-6

Manufactured by Taylor Publishing Company   Dallas, Texas

ESSAY AND GENERAL LITERATURE INDEX REPRINT SERIES

TO

DOCTOR H. J. INGLIS

WITHOUT WHOSE AID A DAMAGED BODY

COULD HARDLY HAVE DEALT WITH

DAMAGED SOULS

Why, all the souls that were were forfeit once;
And He that might the vantage best have took
Found out the remedy.

MEASURE FOR MEASURE

We need to hear the excuses men make to themselves for
their worthlessness.

MARGARET FULLER

PREFACE

Apologies for one's work are usually unprofitable: either it justifies itself, or it does not. Still, I wish to point out that I recognize the extent of the task I have undertaken in the following portraits and the unavoidable inadequacy of the result. The whole of the American Revolution is involved in the background of Benedict Arnold, the whole of the American Revolution and of the French in that of Thomas Paine. Burr and Randolph imply a thorough knowledge of the first quarter of the nineteenth century in the United States, Barnum and Butler, of the third. In the brief time I have had to give I have not been able to increase my familiarity with more than the surface of these interesting and important periods. I have tried to seize and condense what seemed to be essential in the lives and surroundings of the various characters; but I am keenly aware of all the possibilities of misrepresentation and misinterpretation, even when I have been able to escape positive errors of fact, of which I fear there are too many.

In working with printed documents one grows

more and more sceptical as to their reliability, especially when the printing was done more than fifty years ago. Printers were apt to be slipshod. Above all, editors were without a conscientious appreciation of the nature of their task: they did not hesitate to alter, to tone down, to improve, to substitute what they thought a writer should have said for what he did say. Take the Journal of Aaron Burr, as printed by Matthew L. Davis, and compare it with what purports to be the facsimile version published by Mr. Bixby. The liberties of omission, and still worse, of commission, by Davis are astounding. With the Bixby text to fall back upon we can feel that we are getting what Burr really wrote in the Journal; but how about the numerous letters that Davis prints? We have no check upon those, and we can never be sure that we are not dealing with the sentiments and reflections of the editor rather than of the author. The same doubts beset one in regard to Garland's "Randolph." Unless you have a man's own manuscript before your eyes, you can never be quite sure that you are reading what he actually wrote. Such scepticism does not, of course, apply to the admirable editing of Mr. Villard in his "John Brown," or of Mrs. Marshall's collection of the letters of General Butler. But carelessness and indifference do betray

PREFACE

themselves in many places where one would hardly look for them.

This unreliability of printed texts much affects the question of attempting to reproduce original spelling and punctuation in quotations. After considering the matter carefully, I have decided to standardize these matters according to contemporary usage. With spelling so peculiar and characteristic as John Brown's, it seems a pity to do this. But, generally speaking, unless I could collate the original manuscript in every case, which is manifestly impossible, it is useless to reproduce what too often depends upon the careless haste and untrained vision of inexperienced editors.

I have to express my gratitude to many persons who have afforded me valuable assistance in one way or another. Mr. Worthington C. Ford has opened his stores of information to one who would like to appear as grateful as he certainly is needy. The Boston Public Library has kindly allowed me to examine its important John Brown manuscripts. The staff of the Boston Athenæum has assisted me in innumerable ways. My special thanks are due to Mr. M. R. Werner for suggestions in regard to Barnum. I only regret that Mr. Werner's Life of the great showman did not appear in time to be made the basis of my study. But I hope at least that my brief sketch may

PREFACE

call attention to the significance of the striking figure which Mr. Werner has portrayed at length with the thoroughness and elaboration that its typical Americanism deserves. I regret also that my portrait of Randolph was practically completed before the appearance of Mr. William Cabell Bruce's monumental biography of the Virginia statesman. But, although I should like to have drawn more fully upon Senator Bruce's admirable accumulation of material, I hardly feel that my fundamental conception of Randolph's character would have been altered.

GAMALIEL BRADFORD

WELLESLEY HILLS, MASS.

CONTENTS

I
DAMAGED SOULS

DAMAGED SOULS

I
DAMAGED SOULS

THIS is not a book of damned souls, but of damaged souls. Neither you nor I know whether they are damned, and I can't help hoping that every one of them has just a wee chance of heaven.

When it was proposed that I should write a series of biographical studies for "Harper's Magazine," the editor first suggested "iconoclastic portraits": "Our idea would be to go back through our national history and select prominent figures who have loomed over-large in their own day and have shone with a false glory — lucky creatures of chance or of circumstance who appealed tremendously to the popular imagination of their time. . . . Of course, in dealing with such a gallery we should expect you to proceed ruthlessly and with scant deference to tradition." To this proposal I replied that it made "a fascinating appeal to the worst elements of my nature," and that "nothing would amuse me more than to take empty simulacra down from pedestals where they have enjoyed the secure adoration of ages." At the same time I objected that such a work of destruction was not really worth doing, and that in the end it was likely to do more injury to the critic than to the character criticized. I urged that I did not want "to undermine, to overthrow, to destroy, even the things that deserve it," and I pointed out that "in every character I have portrayed so far it has been my endeavor to find the good rather than the evil, to set the figure firmly on its common human basis, but at the same time to insist that if the human heart were not worth loving, my work would not be worth doing." After reflecting on the matter, I made the counter-proposition, to do "a group of somewhat discredited figures, and not endeavor in any way to rehabilitate or whitewash, but to bring out their real humanity and show that, after all, they have something of the same strength and weakness as all of us." And I suggested that the series might pass under the title of "Damaged" or "Patched Souls."

It is true that in this scheme there was from the beginning a certain confusion between damaged souls and damaged reputations. The primary assumption was that the persons dealt with were ill thought of by the world, and it did not necessarily follow that such general reprehension was altogether deserved. At the same time, in all those selected the element of subjective spiritual damage seemed to be quite sufficient to explain, if not to justify, the stigma attached to them, and, as my aim was, not to emphasize the stigma, but to bring out the thoroughly human and even noble and attractive elements, it did not appear that great injustice would be done.

It was quite evident, however, that I was grouping together under a generally opprobrious title, persons whose claims to that bad eminence were of very different quality and degree. The instant that Thomas Paine was announced in a series of damaged souls between two names so popularly reprobated as Benedict Arnold and Aaron Burr the enthusiastic admirers of Paine set up a complaint, that such an insult should be passed upon one of the most conspicuous founders of American Independence. Forgetting the dark horror of Pottawatomie Creek and the subtle taint of fanaticism approaching madness, the lovers of John Brown protested against my classing him with traitors. It was natural that the friends of Randolph should be equally indignant, when they found his genuine, if somewhat erratic, patriotism shadowed in such company. While the families of Barnum and of Butler were likely to object to their being rated as damaged souls at all.

Nevertheless, though in vastly varying measure, I

have felt in all these cases, the more I came to study them, that the general classification was correctly applied. The quality of damage might be very different; but the essential spiritual damage was there. Indeed, I was inclined to think that the mere objective, external damage, the injury inflicted upon others by treasons like those of Arnold and Burr, was a less ineradicable, less damning taint than the inner obliquity or inadequacy, harder to seize and define but even more oppressive to feel, of some others of the group. And I am sure that I personally should have found the loud and vulgar vanity of Paine and Barnum and Butler a far less tolerable housemate than the manly, if misguided, ardor of Arnold, or Burr's incomparable, if fundamentally selfish, personal charm.

And no doubt there is a terrible responsibility in affixing or emphasizing damage in connection with any soul, even those of the dead past, which is not really dead, nor ever can be. One shudders to think of the power wielded by painters of character like Tacitus or Saint-Simon or Clarendon, the power of taking a man out of his quiet grave, where he might have slept with his vices and virtues wrapt peacefully about him, and gibbeting him forever before a gaping posterity in creaking chains of ignominy, perhaps for sins he never committed and errors that existed only in the historian's imagination. And, to be sure, one has not the branding fury of genius that belonged to these mighty masters; yet a bit of mud, even thrown by a feeble hand, has a nasty trick of sticking.

Also, one grows day by day more keenly aware of the insuperable difficulty of coming to final conclusions as to either damage or merit. There is the original difficulty of material. A man of the past can be studied only in what is written by him or about him. What is written by him is not always abundant or always revealing. What is written about him, even by those who knew him well, is reflected and deflected by the recording medium, of which one grows more distrustful, the more one considers it. Even when one has ample material, which can be fairly relied upon, there is the even greater difficulty of interpretation. Supposing that a man really did and said certain things attributed to him, what do those things mean as to his character? Are we justified in generalizing such speech and action to the establishment of certain qualities by which the man may be permanently labeled and classified for posterity? It is evident that the determination of this point requires long training and discipline in the nice analysis and estimate of human motives, and even with such training and discipline, one is likely to err quite as often as to be correct. In fact, the complication and perplexity of the task are so great that one would be a thousand times tempted to abandon it, if its importance were not quite equal to its absorbing fascination. But at least, as one goes on, one learns the lesson of tolerance, of recognizing the certainty of mixed motives for every action, and of inclining more and more to a larger humanity.

As to spiritual damage, the universality of it must also be admitted. Perhaps essentially most of the members of the group here discussed were not much more damaged than the average of their human brothers and sisters. When we come to think over distinguished historical personages, or even Tom, Dick, and Harry, whom we meet daily in the street, some element of imperfection presents itself, which would make it easy to include them in such a list, or even difficult to keep them out. And it is probably the conspicuous stage on which their damage was displayed rather than its fundamental quality which gives some at least of my subjects their claim to a notorious position. Least of all can the writer of such a book claim to be exempt from the damage which he attributes to those whom he discusses. Indeed, he has felt that the surest sign of his own innate depravity was the profound extent to which he sympathized with every one of the souls who came under his pen and the singular tenderness with which they inspired him. The impetuous heroism of Arnold, the noble and sincere idealism of Paine, the cordial, enchanting amiability of Burr, the wayward chivalry of Randolph, the mystical altitude of Brown, even the rollicking good-nature of Barnum, and the robust, rotund, gross humanity of Butler, who could resist them and fail to forget in them for the moment the darker blots and stains? I confess that I could not, and was often forced to the desperate conclusion of Falstaff: "I am bewitched with the rogue's company. If the rascal have not given me medicines to make me love him, I'll be hanged; it could not be else; I have drunk medicines."

It is interesting to trace in these different figures collectively the influence of some of the most marked elements that usually account for spiritual damage. To begin with, there is ambition, the sin by which the angels fell. I do not know that one of our group can be said to have had sufficient largeness of intellect, sufficient intensity of concentrated imaginative power, to have held to one vast goal of success from beginning to end. Brown, with his personal ambition intimately identified with the will of God, perhaps

9

suggests it most. The others were all opportunists, restlessly, eagerly anxious to do great things and win a great place in the world, but leaving the how mainly to the whim of circumstance. Of course they all disclaimed ambition, as we all do, and they were all more or less distracted from it by other considerations, Arnold by passion, Burr by pleasure, Randolph by temper, Barnum and Butler by money. But with every one of them the love of glory was an essential and controlling motive and most of them made it manifest in an idle and misplaced vanity.

Money, again, what a mighty element of spiritual damage it always is. I have already alluded to it with Barnum and Butler, and certainly their names were sufficiently disfigured by it, if not their lives. Paine and Brown I think we may exempt mainly, if not wholly, from the money taint. But avarice discredited the latter days of Randolph, utter financial mismanagement, with its sure train of ruin to others, haunted the whole career of Burr, and it is unnecessary to suggest what money did to Benedict Arnold.

Then there is alcohol, almost as clinging and destructive in its subtle power of ruin as gold. But in our list alcohol was mainly less significant. It may have played some part in the damage of Arnold, but a comparatively slight one. It injured Paine's memory, if not his character. Randolph alone was mastered by it to a serious extent, and even with him alcohol was probably only a secondary agent, working in conjunction with the yet more furious demons of temper and nerves.

And women? Again, it must be said that this usually so fruitful cause of historical damage does not play a predominant part here. Burr alone, of all the seven, was largely notable for sexual irregularity, and even with Burr, it might be suggested that he did a good deal more damage to women than women did to him. The only two women who appear to have exercised any very marked influence in his life were of the noblest strain and of irreproachable character, his wife and his daughter. On the other hand, if there is little for us to study as regards sex influence in the grosser sense, the affection of good women, and the intimate contact with them, not only in the case of Burr, but in those of Arnold and Butler, form a most curious subject for contemplation and analysis. Although we have charming letters of Mrs. Arnold, her hints of feeling as regards her husband are subtle and difficult to disentangle. But Theodosia Burr's devotion to her father is as obvious as it is passionate, and to find a spirit of her noble temper treating as a superior being one who to us seems so peculiarly subject to human frailty affords much matter for reflection. As for Mrs. Butler, her innumerable self-revealing letters, when taken in connection with her husband's career, make one of the most fascinating studies it is possible to imagine. She untwists every fibre of her heart and lays bare all her hopes, all her ambitions, all her passion, all her anguish, with a gift of expression as great as the emotions are intense. Take one characteristic passage, addressed to her husband, which illustrates all the treasures of self-confession these letters enfold: "Now you must not think me vain, that I recall this vision of youth and write it to you; for I lie here so pale and wearied, so unattractive, that I would fain present some bright season of life when I was looked at with pleasure, and *loved*, by those who felt the inspiration of my nature. — Love, that they can never forget while life exists. It came, not from the romance of the school-girl that dies at twenty, but the impassioned woman that art, beauty, and heroic deeds forever stimulate and exult, that cannot fatten from thirty to sixty and waddle through life neglected and self-complaisant."

Yet another cardinal point suggests interesting comparisons between these damaged souls, the question of God. Curiously enough, not one of them was positively and violently irreligious, except Paine, and

even with Paine irreligion was rather a child's frac-
tious rebellion than the thoughtful tragic nihilism
of Lucretius or Schopenhauer. Brown and Barnum,
each in his different way, were earnest Christian believers. Randolph at least tried to be, and Butler
usually wrote as if he were. Arnold referred to God
with a respect which I believe to be genuine, even if
it was sometimes rather remote. Burr took religion
very lightly as he took everything else. It did not become a gentleman to do otherwise. Yet his is the delicious remark, "I think that God is a great deal
better than some people suppose." Altogether, it is
impossible to feel that these damaged souls had any
sense on their own part of being on bad terms with
heaven, however the colder and harsher judgment of
posterity may be inclined to deal with them.

Finally, there is still one other common element
affecting most of the group, and that is their facility,
if not felicity, with words. This does not apply especially to Arnold and Brown, who were above all
things men of action. But the other five were masters
of language, each in his own way. The tongue was
the most vivid and effective thing about them, and
they used it, one and all, with singular and passionate
urgency, to forward their own purposes, to sway men
and women, to achieve the conquest of the world.

And note that they were none of them conscious and deliberate literary artists, except Paine, while even Paine was more interested in the use of his verbal instruments than in the understanding of them. They were all busy, active, practical men, to whom words were tools, no more. But words were ready, handy, terrible tools, and the results these men obtained with them make one more than ever distrustful of the insidious, tremendous, monstrous agency of speech.

Also, almost all our personages were always eager to use their gift of words to enlarge upon themselves, to bring their own achievements and capacities amply before the world. Yet the odd thing is that, with all this limitless discussion of themselves, they seem to have analyzed their own natures and reflected upon their motives very little. They lived for the most part outwardly, expanded, enlarged, engrossed, projected their personalities upon the world about them, and had neither the inclination nor the ability to dissect their own spirits with intense and curious questioning. Randolph is the only considerable exception, and it is interesting to note that with him the spiritual damage was closely related to just this restless analysis of his own soul. The others had, one and all, with regard to themselves, a certain simplicity and almost childlike candor, which one of General

14

Butler's admirers expressed as "single-mindedness," and which, in spite of every damage, undeniably gives to all of them a sort of charm.

But what perhaps impresses and amuses me most with my damaged souls, as I part from them, is the vision of them all gathered together, and the boisterous turmoil of abuse and recrimination with which every one of them would hail all the others. How Butler would storm at Arnold and Burr. With what disgust would Paine regard the mystic Brown, equal almost to the horror of Brown for Paine's indecent ribaldry. While Burr would turn away from Paine and Brown both with quiet contempt, only to find himself coldly shunned by Randolph as a traitor to his country. And the sombre shade of Arnold, avoided by all alike, would yet feel a peculiar shudder of abhorrence at being grouped with the patent, noisy, cheap vulgarity of Barnum.

What would unite them at once, in common forgetfulness of their personal differences, would be the suggestion of me. That an insignificant, impertinent, treacherous biographer should dare to group them under such an infamous title as "Damaged Souls" — the idea would be enough to divert all their wrath from each other and concentrate it on my unfortunate head. And back of the men there are still those three lovely, passionate, devoted women, ready to take up the cause of their idols with far more ardor than even the idols themselves. I see the exquisite, delicate Mrs. Arnold, of the Lawrence portrait, looking at me reproachfully, because I have slandered the general. And Theodosia concedes that I have said some nice things about her father; but why could n't I see him as a superior being as she did? And the delicious Sarah Butler declares that I wormed myself into her confidence only to betray her more cruelly, and she sweeps down upon me with a splendid, histrionic, Shakespearean gesture of contempt. That gesture of contempt haunted me all the time I was writing the portrait of her husband, and I really believe the dread of it made me treat him with more leniency than he deserved.

II
BENEDICT ARNOLD

CHRONOLOGY

Born, Norwich, Connecticut, January 14, 1741.
Enlisted for French and Indian War, 1756.
Married Margaret Mansfield, February 22, 1767.
Commanded expedition to Quebec, autumn of 1775.
Commanded navy on Lake Champlain, autumn of 1776.
Wounded at Saratoga, October 7, 1777.
Commanded in Philadelphia, 1778–1780.
Married Margaret Shippen, April 8, 1779.
Given command at West Point, August, 1780.
Fled to British, September 25, 1780.
Died in London, June 14, 1801.

II
BENEDICT ARNOLD

I

THE complexity of Arnold's tragic adventure is what makes it fascinating and has led so many novelists and dramatists to use him as a central or a subsidiary figure. He was no mean, sneaking, cowardly, consistent rascal. He was a splendid fighter, a quick-eyed soldier, apparently a sincere and earnest patriot, admired and esteemed by thousands of his countrymen, praised and trusted by Washington. Yet he was guilty of the blackest treachery and sold the personal trust of Washington for a cash reward. Could there be a soul more interesting to probe in its subtle mixture of darkness and light?

Arnold's career was one of furious action from his boyhood. Born in 1741, he plunged into the French and Indian War when he was fifteen years old. His early manhood was spent in New Haven, where he married and engaged in several more or less adventurous affairs, by which he accumulated some property. He was active in the Revolution from the start, was with Ethan Allen at Ticonderoga, and managed the first naval enterprise on Lake Champlain.

In the autumn of 1775 he conducted a heroic march
to Quebec and was wounded in the assault upon that
city. In the autumn of 1776 he created a fleet and
fought the battle of Valcour Island. He was slighted
by Congress in the promotion to major-generalships,
to the surprise and disgust of Washington, who repeatedly recommended him. Yet Arnold overlooked
this neglect and took a part in the Saratoga campaign
which won him the enthusiasm of the whole country.
He was incapacitated for field service by a severe
wound and Washington gave him the military governorship of Philadelphia. Here he married his second wife, Margaret Shippen, became intimate with
loyalists, lived extravagantly, was accused of peculation, and irritated the citizens, so that he was finally
tried by a Court Martial. He was acquitted of the
main charges, but was sentenced to be reprimanded
by Washington for minor irregularities. This, with
other complicated considerations, led him to initiate
arrangements with the British, and, after persuading
Washington to entrust him with the command of
West Point, he agreed to deliver it up to the enemy.
Through the arrest of André, who was sent to confer
with him, his intrigues were discovered and he himself barely managed to escape to the British fleet.
He received pay and rank in the British army and

did more or less fighting against his country; but in England he was generally slighted and neglected, and after years of universal failure, he died in 1801, a broken and despairing wreck.

Through all this highly colored and violent life certain good qualities are too obvious to be overlooked or disregarded; yet the hatred inspired by Arnold's end has caused every one of these to be contested and explained away by some one or other of the patriotic historians and biographers. It is exceedingly curious to trace the working of this prejudice in its various details.

To begin with, the man must certainly have had an active and vigorous intelligence. He was not of course a scholar or an abstract thinker. Yet he was at one time a bookseller, among many other things, and must have touched books and had a kind of contact with them. He had a fancy for tag ends of Latin, and his love letters are those of a man who had read the poets and knew how to use them. The papers that he wrote after the betrayal, advising the British as to the conduct of the war, show a large, intelligent grasp of political and military problems, and his technical reports of his own actions have the vigor and simple directness of high intellectual power. Yet his busy detractors have been eager to represent him as a mere muscular swashbuckler, of more tongue than brains.

It is not, however, as a thinker that Arnold is interesting, but as a man who was always eager to go somewhere and do something. He said of himself that "being of an active disposition, and detesting the languor of still life, he relinquished the business of an apothecary."[1] He was quick to relinquish any business that meant keeping still, and his salient, attractive qualities are preëminently those of action and leadership. He liked to command men, to stir them to great actions by his influence and example. No doubt he enjoyed making himself conspicuous in the process; but the love of great things was there.

And beyond question he had some of the finer moral qualities of leadership. He could and did endure privation and misery with his soldiers. He could and did sacrifice his pride, "lays aside his claim and will create no dispute, should the good of the service require them to act in concert," says Washington.[2] He had a large and kindly magnanimity. When he was wounded at Saratoga, one of his men was about to kill the soldier who had wounded him. "Don't hurt him," cried Arnold; "he did but his duty; he is a fine fellow."[3] And his sister says that his soldiers called him "a very humane, tender officer."[4] Yet here, as everywhere, the detraction is zealously at work. It is urged that Arnold was cruel and inhuman. Rather mythical stories are told of his brutality in boyhood, of his tormenting birds and strewing broken glass under the feet of his playmates.[5] It is unfortunately certain that he wrote to Washington — of all men — threatening to revenge any wrongs that might be done to his wife and child "in a deluge of American blood."[6] And if the massacre at Fort Griswold, when Arnold was leading British troops in Connecticut, was not performed by his orders, he, as leader, was responsible for it.

But the cruelty, so far as it existed, was only part of Arnold's intense impulse of executive action. Speed, energy, the immediate realization of any plan, without regard to who suffered — these were his distinguishing characteristics. He had the Herculean physical vigor that in youth could take a mad steer by the nostrils and hold the animal till it was subdued.[7] He had an equally Herculean spiritual vigor, liked difficulties, faced them, challenged them, tore them up by the roots and blotted them out, and waged an ardent, furious conflict with the impossible. This is the kind of thing that inspires men, and Arnold was trusted and beloved, in spite of his dictatorial ways. It is indeed justly urged that he did not carry a single follower into the British lines. But·this only shows the black, hideous, hopeless character of his treason. There is ample evidence that the men who served him believed in his fighting ability and knew that if they followed his banner they would get somewhere, even if they risked everything in the attempt.

And Arnold had not only energy, he had the large conceptions of generalship. As with Washington himself, the pitiful inadequacy of means often blighted these conceptions, or made the success only partial. But the broad grasp was there, all the same. The handling of the Quebec expedition, the management of the Battle of Bemis Heights, so far as Arnold was concerned in it, above all, the naval achievements on Lake Champlain in the autumn of 1776, are substantial evidence. Here, as always, the carping malignancy follows us with tedious iteration. The challenge before the walls of Quebec, which formed the climax of the daring march declared by Jefferson to be equal to Xenophon's retreat, is slighted by some as mere foolish bravado. The critics insist that Arnold was not on the field at Bemis Heights at all, as if the place of the general conducting a battle was in the front fighting rank. And a jealous fellow-officer, General Maxwell, reports of the Champlain battles, "General Arnold, our evil genius to the north, has, with a good deal of industry, got us clear of all our fine fleet." [8] But if one wants an antidote for this querulous fault-finding, one has only to turn to the chapter in Mahan's "Major Operations of the Navies in the War of American Independence" that treats of these same battles on Lake Champlain. For Arnold's treason Mahan's condemnation is as bitter as any one's: but for his generalship, the breadth of his plans, the skill of his conduct in detail, and the magnificent coolness and courage of his personal leadership the naval historian's praise is unstinted. He had made a fleet out of rough boards, he had made fighting sailors out of simple farmers: "Considering its raw material and the recency of its organization, words can scarcely exaggerate the heroism of the resistance, which undoubtedly depended chiefly upon the personal military qualities of the leader." [9] And again: "The little American navy on Lake Champlain was wiped out; but never had any force, big or small, lived to better purpose or died more gloriously." [10] One could hardly say more of Thermopylæ. And Mahan argues that it was this naval resistance of Arnold's that made the Saratoga campaign possible.

Through all these adventures and vicissitudes the one thing that stands out almost undisputed is Arnold's splendid, dashing personal bravery. Even here I have to say "almost," because Wilkinson insinuates that Arnold was drinking freely on the day of Saratoga,[11] and Wayne goes further and declares that he "rarely went in way of danger but when stimulated with liquor, even to intoxication."[12] It may be pointed out that men do not lead great naval battles when drunk. I think Washington would have said with Lincoln that if Arnold drank whiskey, he should like to know the brand. And it is worth observing that in Washington's quiet comments on his leading generals he questions whether both Wayne and Wilkinson are not too friendly to the bottle.[13] But any "almost" as to Arnold's love of fighting and his dashing, reckless exposure of limb and life may be disregarded. Not that he was wholly reckless. In his ardent youth he led an attack against the house of a well-known Tory, Dr. Peters. Peters threatened to shoot if his assailants advanced a step further, and Arnold retired. "I am no coward," he said; "but I know Dr. Peters's disposition. . . . I have no wish for death at present."[14] Still, what one thinks of most is the self-forgetful daring which in boyhood threw itself on the whirling water-wheel and was dashed gasping over and over through the depths, and which again at Saratoga, after Gates's jealousy had deprived it of all official command, rushed upon the field and inspired the troops to the desperate charges which filled friend and enemy alike with admiring enthusiasm.

Again and again in a retreat Arnold was the last to leave by land or sea. Vanity, say his detractors. Perhaps it was vanity; but war can put up with a lot of vanity of that description. Heroism breeds heroism, and the feeling of Arnold's men is best shown in the words of one of them: "He was our fighting general, and a bloody fellow he was. He did n't care for nothing, he'd ride right in. It was 'Come on, Boys' — 't was n't 'Go, boys.' He was as brave a man as ever lived."[15]

II

THE fine qualities of Arnold's character above analyzed are too plainly offset by serious and glaring defects, and it is natural that the taint of his great guilt should swell these to a cloud of obloquy. His was a nature of strong and masterful impulses, insufficiently balanced by any groundwork of principle or moral habit. Not that his education had been neglected in this respect. He had a pious and devoted mother, whose earnest letters to him have been preserved. "Pray, my dear," she writes with pathetic foresight, "don't neglect your precious soul, which once lost can never be regained." [16] Arnold himself shows no sign of irreligion or any tendency to base irregularities of life upon irregularities of theology. Without the slightest trace of cant, he has occasional reverent phrases which seem to indicate a decided religious habit of thought: "This disaster, though unfortunate at first view, we must think a very happy circumstance on the whole, and a kind interposition of Providence." [17]

But whatever moral basis there was, it was too weak to maintain control in a temper played upon constantly by furious passions, and we read Arnold best when we think of these as making him the sport of their tempestuous violence. Lying? He was naturally frank, genuine, straightforward, was too proud to be anything else. Yet the strange complications of his career probably made him careless of strict veracity, even before the climax of his guilt involved him in its fatal snare of dissimulation. Drink? He certainly was no habitual drunkard; yet when he was twenty-five the sheriff had orders to arrest him "for drunkenness and being disabled in the use of his understanding and reason." [18] Ambition? Often a virtue as much as a fault and the mother of great and noble actions, but in natures ill-regulated as Arnold's apt to run riot in strange and disorderly paths. There were times when he disclaimed it. When all the world seemed to be against him, he made up his mind to buy a farm and retire into rural oblivion, declaring that his ambition was to be "a good citizen rather than shining in history." [19] The mood did not last, and his normal attitude is probably better represented by his explanation to Joshua Smith as to his youth: "Determined to be the *faber suæ fortunæ*, he lost no opportunity that offered, and when they did not take notice of him, he courted them by all honest exertions to advance his fortunes." [20]

And, alas, the baser elements of ambition were more prominent in this fiery spirit than the nobler. There was a sensitiveness as to his rank and dignity, which was sometimes subdued, but too often triumphed. And there was an ardent, a cruel, a selfish vanity such as is too ready to prostitute great causes to petty ends. Not that Arnold was a braggart in words or generally inclined to indulge in frivolous rhodomontade. On the contrary, his letters and reports are usually simple and dignified. But the taint went deeper and showed in an incurable desire to play the chief rôle, not only to do great and significant actions, but to get the credit of having done them.

Especially in the more advanced stage of his career

this vanity took a social form. "He was almost insane with social ambition," says Mr. Fisher.[21] This is too strong. But it is true that, when he found himself at the head of the government in Philadelphia, in the midst of an old and aristocratic society, the impulse to cut a great figure was nearly irresistible. Hence arose the worst of his money troubles, which probably had more than anything else to do with his final fall.

It was, I think, the love of display and the desire to assert his great position that led to Arnold's extravagance, rather than any ingrained fondness for luxury and self-indulgence. No doubt he liked these things; but he had been too inured to hardship to be dependent upon them. There is no evidence that he had been an abundant spender in his youth. Nor was he, as has been sometimes charged, avaricious. There are authentic instances of his ready generosity, most notable among them being his thoughtful provision for the children of General Warren, to whom he sent five hundred dollars, with the promise of further assistance, which was not forgotten.[22]

But he was a bad financial manager, he had great needs, and all his life his sanguine temperament led him into dubious speculation, from which the path to dishonesty is too easy to travel. "In view of the light afterwards thrown upon his character, it is not unlikely that he may sometimes have availed himself of his high position to aid these speculations," says Fiske.[23] At any rate, his enemies thought so, and said so. Arnold himself bitterly resented the charge: "I cannot but think it extremely cruel, when I have sacrificed my ease, health, and a great part of my private property in the cause of my country, to be calumniated as a robber and a thief."[24] And when the matter was brought to formal trial, he was explicitly exonerated from wrong-doing. It must be remembered that in the complicated conditions of a great war many public officials are apt to be involved in the appearance of irregularity and everybody tends to become suspicious of everybody else. Nevertheless, where suspicion attaches to a man so constantly as to Arnold, and where the other circumstances of his career so strongly favor it, it is difficult not to accept it as in part founded upon fact.

It is sometimes urged that Arnold's extravagance was caused by that of his second wife, Margaret Shippen. This is unjust in that the general's wanton display began before his marriage and that Mrs. Arnold showed herself in later years an excellent manager. At the same time, she had been accustomed to comfort, and comfort is a costly thing, and it

31

brought huge pressure upon her husband, and he loved her: which has been the story of many men's ruin. Among the passions that rioted in Arnold's restless heart love and hate were certainly not the least. What his general relations with women were we have no direct means of knowing. It is not probable that he was a man like Aaron Burr, to make the possession of some woman or other a constant interest of his life. His nature was too violently active for this. He would have said with Enobarbus, of the loveliest of women, "It were pity to cast them away for nothing, though, between them and a great cause, they should be esteemed nothing." But when he loved, he loved intensely. That he also loved thoughtfully and tenderly is shown by his sister's description of him as, loverlike, "tormenting himself with a thousand fancied disasters which have happened to you and the family," [25] and the minute directions which he sent to Mrs. Arnold for her journey to West Point, when he was in the midst of the tumult of the betrayal. Whether he himself loved or not, he was deeply beloved. It does not appear from his portraits that he was strikingly handsome; but no doubt his manly vigor and energy were of a sort to affect the feminine heart. In any case, the exquisite devotion of at least three noble women, his mother, his sister, and his wife, should suffice to prove that there was something in him not wholly unlovable.

The most piquant feature of Arnold's love-making is his letters. In the spring of 1778, when he was a widower thirty-seven years old, he wished to marry Elizabeth DeBlois, of Boston, and wrote her passionate letters, declaring that his whole happiness depended upon her consent. Take one sample of the quality of his wooing: "Friendship and esteem founded on the merit of the object is the most certain basis to build a lasting happiness upon, and when there is a tender and ardent passion on one side and friendship and esteem on the other, the heart must be callous to every tender sentiment if the taper of love is not lighted up at the flame." [26] Just six months later this undying affection, which had been declined by Miss DeBlois, was transferred to Miss Shippen and expressed itself with the same transport and, mind you, in the very identical words given above. Now what do you make of that? I cannot explain it. Was the fellow a Lovelace, cynically convinced that one cheap artifice of Eros would suffice for all women alike? Or was he simply a busy, middle-aged man who thought that ladies liked to have nice things said to them and, having got one convenient model, perhaps from the complete letter-writer, used it to serve every turn? I incline to the latter hypothesis; but one cannot help thinking of the remark of Mrs. Page to Mrs. Ford, in the "Merry Wives of Windsor": "He hath a thousand of these letters, sure more, and these are of the second edition."

Artificial or not, the wooing seemed to answer with Miss Shippen, who was many years younger than her wooer. Her father's dislike of the match only stimulated her affection, till her health failed under the strain, and the parental veto was withdrawn. As Weir Mitchell, the greatest nerve specialist of his day, observed about the case: "When a delicate-minded, sensitive, well-bred woman falls in love with a strong, coarse, passionate man, there is no more to be said except 'take her.'" [27] The two were married in April, 1779, though Arnold was still so crippled by his wound that "during the marriage ceremony [he] was supported by a soldier, and when seated his disabled limb was propped upon a camp-stool." [28]

If love was a large element in Arnold's life, hate was a larger. Not that he entertained long, cruel grudges and remote vengeance. His nature was too straightforward for that. But his quick, violent temper was moved to anger on any fancied provocation of slight or insult, and his whole history is an incredible succession of unprofitable quarrels. His loving mother begged him in his youth to keep a "steady watch over your thoughts, words, and actions." [29] Alas, alas, how soon the tender injunctions of mothers are forgot!

These bitter and more or less disreputable conflicts abound with Arnold, from almost our earliest record until the end. Three duels we know of, and there were probably many others. His own description of one more ruffianly encounter sets the tone: "I took the liberty of breaking his head, and on his refusing to draw like a gentleman . . . I kicked him very heartily and ordered him from the point immediately." [30] He quarreled with his inferiors, quarreled with colonels, captains, privates, and citizens. He quarreled with his superiors, Gates who had befriended him, Reed the President of the Executive Council of Pennsylvania, with disastrous results. No doubt the fault was not always on one side; but such a luxury of altercation makes one suspicious. Quarrels to him seem to have been the zest of life. They fill his portrait with dark shadows and ugly corners.

And back of the quarrels was the abnormal, uneasy, quivering sense of his own importance. This is excellently suggested in the remark of Washington: "He received a rebuke before I could convince him of the impropriety of his entering upon a justification of his conduct in my presence, and for bestowing such illiberal abuse as he seemed disposed to do upon those whom he denominated his persecutors." [31] Alas, he was too ready to see persecutors everywhere. If he could only have remembered the admirable words of Orlando, himself a good fighter, when it came to the push! "I will chide no breather in the world but myself, against whom I know most faults." Arnold was riddled with faults, and must have known it; yet he seemed ready to chide every breather that lived.

III

AND now we are somewhat better able to understand the critical action of Arnold's life. Yet even so, the horror of it is almost inexplicable: to sell a sacred trust and the confidence of a personal benefactor for a cash reward. In the words of Mahan, who so greatly admired his heroism and soldiership: "It is not the least of the injuries done to his nation in after years, that he should have . . . effaced this glorious record by so black an infamy." [32]

What interests us, of course, is not so much the fact, as the motives behind it, especially Arnold's own view of those motives. To use the apt phrase of Margaret Fuller: "We need to hear the excuses men make to themselves for their worthlessness." [33] And in every such critical decision of life, as in the minor ones also, there is a vast complication of motives, which we too often fail to realize. We are inclined to simplify the motives of others and especially to overlook many elements in our own. Above all is this true in a nature of fierce action like Arnold's, which generally has neither the leisure nor the disposition to spend much time upon self-analysis. In the records that we have of his earlier life I do not find indications of such analysis, nor do I believe that it was there to any great extent. It does not seem possible that a man of large imaginative habit could have failed to picture to himself the terrible consequences of the step he was taking. Yet, on the other hand, a very vivid imagination will sometimes be content to frame a wide possibility of contingencies and then dwell only upon those that are agreeable.

Of one thing we may be sure, that Arnold never admitted to himself that he was a scoundrel or that his motives were villainous. There may be deliberate rascals who do this; but I am sure he was not one of them. When he wrote to Elizabeth DeBlois that the love with which she had inspired him could not "admit of an unworthy thought or action," [34] I believe he was absolutely sincere. His most bitter critic,

Stevens, declares that "there is no evidence that the heart of Arnold ever beat with one patriotic thrill." [35] This is absurd. His heart had as many such thrills as three quarters of the men who fought in the Revolution. When he said, "No public or private injury or insult shall prevail on me to forsake the cause of my injured and oppressed country, until I see peace and liberty restored to her, or nobly die in the attempt," [36] he meant it, as much as most men mean such words. When he called one who was doing precisely what he did later, "a most plausible and artful villain," [37] he meant it. When he wrote to Washington, "the heart which is conscious of its own rectitude, cannot attempt to palliate a step which the world may censure as wrong," [38] when he wrote of his sons in later years that they were "possessed of strict principles of honor and integrity," [39] as if they had derived them from him, he was absolutely sincere in what he said.

Nevertheless, he did what other men consider a treacherous, hideous, abominable deed. How did he do it, and why? We must look first at the general conditions which affected him. There is no doubt that in 1779 and 1780 there was much discouragement and weariness, and a number of persons inclined to the opinion that Arnold suggested when he said to Joshua Smith that "the private interests of a few leading individuals seemed to him to be more the object contemplated in protracting the war ... than the good of his fellow-citizens." [40] The British were persistent, the French alliance was distasteful, Congress was incapable and torn by factions, the resources of the country were scanty, at any rate ill managed. Washington himself said, "I have almost ceased to hope." [41] Arnold in Philadelphia, surrounded by people of Tory leaning, received all these dark impressions with double force. It was asserted by Aaron Burr and his biographers [42] that Mrs. Arnold emphasized this tendency in her husband and was indeed an active participant in his guilt. As a matter of fact, her innocence seems beyond dispute; but her sympathies and those of her friends were no doubt important elements in the great decision.

Even more pressing were the considerations personal to Arnold himself. There was the odious matter of money. His debts were piled up, his claims upon Congress were still unsettled, cash must be got from somewhere. Just what sum he bargained to surrender West Point for cannot be definitely determined. Thirty thousand pounds was the legendary figure. [43] As he could not keep his agreement, he received some six thousand pounds in what he must have felt to be very inadequate compensation for all his losses.[44] The incurably sordid view here involved peeps out in his remark to Smith, just before the treason was consummated: "Smith, here am I now, after having fought the battles of my country, and find myself with a ruined constitution, and this limb ... now rendered useless to me. At the termination of this war, where can I seek for compensation for such damages as I have sustained?"[45]

But no doubt he preferred to dwell upon the base ingratitude which disregarded his losses, rather than upon the financial importance of them. The intense sensitiveness as to rank and advancement, which is apparently more marked in the military profession than in any other, was as prominent in the Revolution as in the Civil War and at other times. Generals Greene, Sullivan, and Knox all threatened to resign on the same day, because it was reported that an inferior and undistinguished officer was to receive promotion.[46] In a passionate and prejudiced temperament like Arnold's the slights inflicted upon him worked like maddening poison. "I daily discover so much baseness and ingratitude among mankind that I almost blush at being of the same species," he writes to Miss Shippen, just before his marriage.[47] And the remedy he found was to display on his own part a

baseness and ingratitude that no one could surpass.

Yet he probably persuaded himself that he was to
be the savior of his country. As one of his biographers
ingeniously points out,[48] he may have argued that
his treachery would never be discovered, but that
West Point would be taken, the Confederacy would
fall, the British supremacy would be restored, and he
himself would be a prominent figure in the dazzling
future of America. As he expressed it to Germain,
"I was intent to have demonstrated my zeal by an
act, which, had it succeeded as intended, must have
immediately terminated the unnatural convulsions
that have so long distracted the Empire." [49] The example of General Monk appears to have been much
in Arnold's mind and the immensely significant part
played by him in bringing about the English Restora-
tion. Such a rôle as this teased and tickled his vanity,
till it grew to be an obsession.

So the great betrayal came about. It was no sudden
impulse of whirlwind vengeance. For a year and a
half Arnold was in correspondence with Sir Henry
Clinton, first vaguely and anonymously, gradually
with greater definiteness. He at length prevailed
upon Washington to entrust him with West Point
and then deliberately arranged to surrender it. The

negotiations, toward the climax, were complicated. André was deputed to confer with Arnold personally. They met on September 22, 1780, and discussed matters without witnesses. But André, in attempting to return, was captured with his compromising papers. Colonel Jameson, to whom he was taken, blunderingly sent word to Arnold, instead of to Washington. The latter had been prevented from breakfasting with the Arnolds, as he expected to do. He sent his aides in advance, and they were all seated at the table, when the message from Jameson was delivered. Arnold, with marvelous self-control, made no sign but quietly excused himself. When Mrs. Arnold followed him, he broke the news to her, left her completely prostrated, flung himself upon the first horse obtainable, rode to the river by what is still called Arnold's path, entered his barge, displayed a flag of truce, and made his escape to the British vessels in safety, leaving André to suffer the degrading death of spy. Arnold went uncompanioned, with not one single follower to make his desertion valuable. The treason had failed. The consummation of his long efforts and tortuous devices, of his strangled conscience and ruined peace, was pitiable disaster. What was there left in life for him?

The storm of horror and contempt that burst behind him has rarely been equaled in the history of human execration. His old companions in arms disowned him with disgust. "From all I can learn Arnold is the greatest villain that ever disgraced human nature," wrote Greene.[50] Wayne was even more emphatic: "The dirty, dirty acts which he has been capable of committing beggar all description." [51] Varick, his own aide de camp, could only insist upon "his mean and dirty peculation and embezzlement of public property." [52] Worst of all was Washington: "He seems to have been so hackneyed in villainy and so lost to all sense of honor and shame, that, while his faculties will enable him to continue his sordid pursuits, there will be no time for remorse." [53]

IV

No fifth act of a tragedy was ever more impressively moral than the last twenty years of Arnold's life. The interesting thing is that we have not one authentic, direct, intimate word of his own, describing his emotions and experiences; for the formal address explaining his action to his American fellow-citizens, issued soon after he escaped, cannot be said to throw much light upon the man's soul. It is easy for our imaginations to supply him with psychological states. Colonel Laurens wrote to Washington that Arnold must be undergoing agony, and Washington, in replying with the words quoted above, denied this: "I am mistaken if, at *this* time [October, 1780] 'Arnold is undergoing the torments of a mental hell.' He wants feeling." [54] This may have been true then, may have been true later. We cannot prove or disprove it: we can only deduce possibilities from external facts.

The facts certainly indicate that Arnold's life was not a comfortable one. During the months that he remained in America, commanding British armies, the abuse of him on the American side was unbounded, and the harshness with which he exercised his authority did not tend to mitigate the hatred of his former countrymen. Perhaps the most vivid illustration of this is the often told story of the prisoner who was asked by Arnold what the Americans would do to him, if he were captured. "They will cut off that shortened leg of yours wounded at Quebec and at Saratoga, and bury it with all the honors of war, and then hang the rest of you on a gibbet." [55]

Nor were the experiences in England much more agreeable. The practical side of life was a constant struggle. The king granted a pension to Mrs. Arnold; but their means were insufficient to maintain the style of living they were accustomed to. Arnold endeavored to obtain opportunities for military advancement and distinction; but his urgency was disregarded. To supply his financial needs he was driven to all sorts of speculation, notably the hazardous equipping of privateers, and his ventures were always tormenting and usually unsuccessful. Socially he fared little better. The court was kind to him. But the world at large was cold. The Whigs were bitter, the Tories mainly indifferent. Open slights were not uncommon. One insult from Lord Lauderdale was so offensive that Arnold met it with a challenge. A duel resulted, in which the general bore himself with a good deal of credit. If we are to believe Mrs. Arnold, the affair greatly improved his social situation: "It has been highly gratifying to find the General's conduct so much applauded, which it has been universally, and particularly by a number of the first characters in the Kingdom, who have called upon him in consequence of it." [56]

But these are the words of wifely attachment, and the most charming, the most assuaging aspect of the strange tragedy of Arnold's later years is the tenderness of his young and lovely wife, the enfolding, sustaining affection that shines like a delicate, pale star in the chaos of utter ruin. After the disaster at West Point Mrs. Arnold for a time sought refuge with her father in Philadelphia. Here she was regarded with

45

suspicion and dislike; and she was finally compelled to join her husband, first meeting him in New York, and then following him to England. Through all the vicissitudes of his sojourn there her thoughtfulness, her devotion never failed, and they are beautifully reflected in the multitude of her letters that have been preserved by her family. In threading the thorny tangle of Arnold's finances her prudence, discretion, and foresight seem to have been admirable. She liked comfort, she liked luxury, she liked to stand well with the world. But she liked honesty and independence better, and she toiled courageously and wearily to maintain them.

Her affection for her children, her solicitude for their welfare and their future, were untiring. She writes repeatedly and anxiously to her father as to the provision to be made for them. And her loving care and watchfulness for the children of her husband's first marriage were almost as great as for her own.

But what is most interesting in Mrs. Arnold's letters, and what most concerns us, is the delicate divination of her feeling for her husband and his for her. As to the latter we have only the reflection in her correspondence. It has been argued from one passage, "Years of unhappiness have past, I had cast my lot, complaints were unavailing, and you and my

46

other friends are ignorant of the many causes of uneasiness I have had,"[57] that her husband was un-
faithful to her. It may have been so. Unfaithfulness
was in his nature. At any rate, I am sure that he
turned again and again to the infinite solace of those
comforting arms and of that tender, sheltering heart.
The complete trust shown by his making her his
executrix and giving her the whole charge of his
affairs[58] only bears out the pathos of her plaint for
"the loss of a husband whose affection for me was
unbounded."[59]

As for her affection for him, it is impossible to
question its depth or permanence, however it may be
veiled under her noble and sensitive reserve. She
showed it even in the confused misery of the first
revelation at West Point. "At present," writes Hamilton, who was with her, "she almost forgets his
crime in his misfortunes; and her horror at the guilt
of the traitor is lost in her love of the man."[60] She
showed it during the long dragging years in England
by her desire to maintain his position and support his
credit. She showed it by her intense solicitude when
he was absent or in danger, as when she speaks of
her anxiety "for the fate of the best of husbands"[61]
and when she depicts the terrible day of the Lauderdale duel: "What I suffered for near a week is not to

47

be described; the suppression of my feelings, lest I should unman the General, almost at last proved too much for me; and for some hours my reason was despaired of." [62] Yet even here her first thought was for her husband's reputation: "Weak woman as I am, I would not wish to prevent what would be deemed necessary to preserve his honor." [63] And most touching and pathetic of all I find her desperate determination to keep his name unstained in the recollection of his children. In speaking of his over-solicitude for their future, she says: "But the solicitude was in itself so praiseworthy, and so disinterested, and never induced him to deviate from rectitude, that his children should ever reverence his memory." [64] O immortal tenderness of woman's love, which could insist fearlessly upon the rectitude of Benedict Arnold!

But even love like this could not make those English years anything but hell, or save that pitiable life from being a melancholy ruin. Though Arnold tells us nothing himself, one or two anecdotes preserve some evidence of what his misery must have been. There is a family tradition that when he was near death, he caused his old Continental uniform to be brought to him and put it on, muttering, "God forgive me for ever putting on any other." [65] More reliable and authentic is the incident related by Talleyrand in his Memoirs. Meeting a stranger, who, he was told, was an American general, in a little inn at Falmouth, Talleyrand made various inquiries. The stranger was far from responsive; and finally, on being pressed for introductions to persons at home, he explained: "I am perhaps the only American who cannot give you letters for his own country.... All the relations I had there are now broken.... I must never return to the States." "He dared not tell me his name," adds Talleyrand. "It was General Arnold. I must confess that I felt much pity for him, for which political puritans will perhaps blame me, but with which I do not reproach myself, for I witnessed his agony." [66] Could there be a more hopeless abyss of human fate than to be pitied for dishonesty by Talleyrand? The scoundrel who succeeded pitying the scoundrel who failed. Finally there is the story of Arnold, accompanied by a lady, visiting Westminster Abbey and pausing to look upon the monument of André. [67] And this, in its dumb significance, is to me the most tragic of all. What an enormous tempest of grief that contemplation must have carried with it: the man whose life he had destroyed for nothing, or only for the ruin of his own; the man whose life he might have saved by a heroic sacrifice which would almost have blotted out his crime. The legend ran in the British army that Arnold offered to give himself up for André, but was prevented by Clinton.[68] If so, it was a cruel bit of kindness. To have given his life for André's would have averted those bitter years, would have gone far to redeem his name from infamy, would have saved him from having to change the proud motto of his earlier day, *gloria sursum*, glory above all things, to the sad legend which he adopted at last, *nil desperandum*, only too aptly to be mistranslated: nothing but despair.

III
THOMAS PAINE

CHRONOLOGY

Born, Thetford, England, January 29, 1737.
Became a master stay-maker at Sandwich, 1759.
Married Mary Lambert, September 27, 1759.
Wife died, 1760.
Married Elizabeth Ollive, March 26, 1771.
Separated from wife, 1774.
Sailed for America, 1774.
"Common Sense" published, January 10, 1776.
"The American Crisis" published from 1776 to 1783.
Sailed for France, 1787.
"The Rights of Man," Part I, published, 1791.
Member of Convention, 1792.
Wrote "The Age of Reason," Part I, 1793.
Imprisoned in Paris, 1793.
Letter to Washington, 1796.
Founded Church of Theophilanthropy, 1797.
Returned to America, 1802.
Died, New York, June 8, 1809.

III
THOMAS PAINE

I

Oн, what fun it is to be a rebel: to shatter, scatter, tear down, and destroy, and let others worry about building up again; or, if you like, to frame cloud fancies of possible utopias and then brand the dull things of earth who will not let you make such fancies real.

.The first half of the eighteenth century was an age of convention, in both good and bad senses, convention in politics, in manners, in thought, in art, in morals. There is nothing like convention to breed rebels, and the last half of the eighteenth century, with the first years of the nineteenth, is a fruitful time for studying the type. The rebel hates control, restraint, limit, demands and delights in the free, abundant exercise of his own will, his own ardent sense of initiative and personality. He likes to assert himself, to make others feel that there is something there to assert: it affords him a concrete assurance of the fact, which is comforting; and it appears that nothing gives us more evidence of our own stability and reality than to destroy something else. The rebel has a splendid, joyous confidence in his own convictions, believes that his bright, glittering reason was given him to hew and cut and thrust through all that seems to him sham, pretense, and old, worm-eaten, time-consecrated falsity. He pursues his triumphant, disastrous way, untroubled by the criticism and abuse of spite and malice, indeed rather stimulated by them; and his royal self-assurance is rarely disturbed by the subtle intrusion of sceptical humor: if he has humor, it turns him from a rebel into something else. Finally, the rebel, at his best, is saved by a passionate enthusiasm for humanity. He wants to make the world over. Of course the way to do this is to begin by turning it upside down. The great ideal rebels are Satan and Prometheus, though perhaps the human enthusiasm was a little more evident in the latter.

Thomas Paine was essentially a rebel. As Mr. Sedgwick puts it, "Wherever revolution was, there was Paine also,"[1] and Mr. Sedgwick elsewhere quotes Paine's noble reply to Franklin, who said, "Where liberty is, there is my country," "Where liberty is not, there is mine."[2] It is true that Paine had not the dignity of Prometheus, nor the picturesqueness of Satan; neither had he the piquant, romantic cynicism of Voltaire, Iago, and Mephistopheles, who perhaps were not rebels, but critics; he was just a commonplace rebel, entirely practical, a trifle sordid, and altogether English.

Paine was born at Thetford, England, in 1737. His father was a Quaker, of rather humble station, and the boy was but slightly educated. Up to middle life his existence was humdrum and insignificant: two wives lost, by death and separation, little means, little comfort, and no glory. In 1774 he came to America, at the prompting of Franklin, and made his pen a vigorous agent in the American Revolution. He returned to England, wrote "The Rights of Man" and stirred up this world, went to France, mingled in the French Revolution as a member of the Convention, was shut up in prison by fiercer rebels than himself, and there wrote "The Age of Reason" and stirred up the other world. Monroe got him out of his difficulties, he was reinstated in the Convention, but achieved little further in France. In 1802 he returned to America, found himself, to his surprise and disgust, at odds with American respectability, and died in 1809, practically unfriended and forlorn, though by no means forgotten.

Paine's enthusiasm, when he arrived in America, after being drenched for nearly forty years in English obscurity and penury, reminds one of Matthew

Arnold's remark: "When the dissenter first lands in America, he thinks he is in heaven." Curiously enough, Paine himself quotes a similar saying by "one of the richest manufacturers in England": "England, Sir, is not a country for a dissenter to live in, — we must go to France." [3] The man's delight, his ecstasy over this new-found paradise are really touching: "The scene which that country presents to the eye of a spectator, has something in it which generates and encourages great ideas." [4] The natural surroundings are inexhaustible in richness, incomparable in beauty. The people are comfortable, contented, happy, untrammeled by old traditions, unvexed by old exactions. They have shaken off the past, they look forward, and when they look forward, every prospect pleases with the promise of a world which may be shaped and moulded to all the dream perfections that any rebel ever imagined.

Though he had made only a few unimportant attempts at writing in England, the charm of this outlook and his gratitude for being offered a share in it made Paine an author, and his pamphlet, "Common Sense," printed early in 1776 and followed at intervals by the various numbers of "The American Crisis," stirred and spurred his new fellow-countrymen far more actively on the road to freedom than any other words produced by tongue or pen, unless the actual Declaration of Independence. Neither these writings nor anything in Paine's later life indicate a gift for practical statesmanship or concrete administration; but his words burn everywhere with a large and splendid ardor for democratic ideals, for liberty, equality, and opportunity for every one, and he was especially happy in insisting upon just the points that were essential in that critical stage of American affairs. When all men were hesitating over the audacity of final separation from Britain, he spoke right out: why palter? why delay? Be free, set up for yourselves, a great destiny is before you, show yourselves worthy of it. He preached nationality, coördination, coöperation, that the people should feel that they were a people and should grow strong in that consciousness. He preached federal union, that petty jealousies and local narrowness should be forgotten, "Our great title is Americans — our inferior one varies with the place." [5] It was Thomas Paine who first used the words that now echo over the whole world, "The United States of America." [6]

For he had a wonderful power of building phrases, of shaping swift, sharp sentences that should pierce dull ears and dead hearts and make them throb and thrill and work and live. He began his first Crisis paper, "These are the times that try men's souls," and few words have been oftener or more aptly repeated. He had a surprising, startling vigor of intense, direct utterance that made the most inert feel that he must do something. And of course he sometimes overshot himself, let the fury of his pen betray him into violence and unnecessary insult. England? He was said to hate England. He did not hate England, but he did hate some English ways of doing things: "It was equally as much from her manners as from her injustice that she lost the colonies," he remarks shrewdly.[7] King George? He was a "Royal Brute," which disposes of him.[8] Tories? "Every Tory is a coward."[9]

But, human nature being what it is, it must be admitted that even these extravagances added to the effect of Paine's pamphlets. And the effect was enormous. "Common Sense" was sold by the hundred thousand.[10] "Every living man in America in 1776, who could read, read 'Common Sense,'" wrote Theodore Parker.[11] Even the discreet Trevelyan is hurried into superlatives on the subject: "It would be difficult to name any human composition which has had an effect at once so instant, so extended, and so lasting."[12]

The consequence of all this was at first naturally

58

an immense admiration and enthusiasm for Thomas
Paine, a general applause that might have turned
any man's head. He was given the degree of Master
of Arts by the University of Pennsylvania,[13] which
to an English mechanic must have meant something.
The sober and judicious Franklin spoke of "Common Sense" as having "prodigious effects."[14] Washington, whose opinions were always moderate and
well-weighed, commented on "the sound doctrine
and unanswerable reasoning contained in the pamphlet,"[15] and found it "working a powerful change
there in the minds of many men";[16] and he was so
impressed with the trumpet exhortation of the first
"Crisis" that he ordered it generally read to his dis-
pirited army.[17] Paine's merit was also practically
recognized by Congress, which elected him secretary
of its Committee of Foreign Affairs, an office which he
held for nearly two years. When he returned to England, he was almost equally admired in the more
liberal English circles. He dined with dukes and
visited them. He was lauded and, what was perhaps
even more complimentary, he was feared. When he
crossed to France, then in the earlier agonies of the
Revolution, he was welcomed as a divine messenger.
Here was the man who had established liberty in the
new world; why could he not do as much in the old?

And as a later but overwhelming climax, Napoleon told him "that a statue of gold ought to be erected to him *in every city in the universe;* he also assured Paine that he always slept with a copy of 'The Rights of Man' under his pillow, and conjured him to honor him with his counsel and advice." [18]

II

WHICH was all rather too smooth sailing for a rebel. But by the time Napoleon came to praise, Paine's popularity in America had greatly fallen off. His well-meant but indiscreet interference, during his secretaryship, in the financial tangle of Silas Deane first somewhat shook public confidence in him. And as he went on with his later political and finally with his religious writings, the general attitude changed from extreme enthusiasm to a bitterness, a contempt, a hearty repudiation, which lasted for a century at least, is hardly now forgotten, and would be difficult to surpass in the history of human prejudice. With a prophetic instinct he himself described the possibility of this change in general, "It so often happens that men live to forfeit the reputation at one time they gained at another"; [19] but he could hardly have foreseen how complete the reversal would be in his own case. In England he was tried for sedition. In

America, bitterest irony of all, he was refused the right to vote as an American citizen. And the fierce invective of Cobbett will serve as an illustration of the abuse which the world long heaped upon one who supposed he had done it service: "There he lies, manacled, besmirched with filth, crawling with vermin, loaded with years and infamy.[20] ... Like Judas he will be remembered by posterity; men will learn to express all that is base, malignant, treacherous, unnatural, and blasphemous by the single monosyllable, Paine." [21]

When one examines Paine's writings in the light of the changes that have taken place since his time, it is difficult to find anything in his general principles that accounts for all this storm of obloquy. As regards politics, he seems to have urged many of the reforms, generally considered beneficial, which are now so much accepted that we cannot imagine the world without them. It is the hard fate of rebels to be sooner or later looked upon as mere conservatives by those who succeed them in the same line of activity, and even Paine did not entirely escape this misfortune. He was unwilling to go the later lengths of the French Revolution. He reiterates his firm adherence to the principle of private property.[22] In many of his political ideas he is nobly and broadly constructive;

and though there is a great deal of vague talk about "rights," such as always tickled eighteenth-century ears, the rights that are asserted are such as one must sympathize with, whether one considers them wholly practical or not. How much of this talk Paine got from Rousseau and others, and how much he spun out of his own brain, will never be settled. He himself insisted on his originality, and in some points, like finance, his independence of view is evident. But it is probable that the ideas that were so widely spread around him had permeated his thought more than he imagined. The immense, insinuating influence of Rousseau is apparent here as elsewhere.

Yet, though the construction in Paine is obvious and undeniable, the destruction is more obvious still, indulged in with even more relish and carried on at all times with all the rebel's intense and unremitting vigor. Construction is so difficult, involves such painful thought, is at best so pervious to criticism. Destruction is so easy. You have only to flourish your pen, and kings and crowns totter — on paper, at any rate. Let us throw over those old relics, get rid of tyranny, get rid of aristocracy, get rid of government, if you push us. What is government anyway, but a device of the devil to override the sacred natural instincts and the lovely primitive kindliness of man?

And this dangerous, treacherous pen does slip so easily into violence and abuse. Paine could frame noble compliment and eulogy; but he could also write bitter, savage, cruel, contemptible sentences, sentences the bitterness of which was sure to damage their author more than any one else. This tendency to bitterness grew with age, perhaps naturally. There was plenty of such writing in the last years of the eighteenth century, and others may have been much worse than Paine; but Paine was bad enough. The "Letters to American Citizens" are brutal and disgusting. The "Letter to Washington," written after Paine's release from the French prison, from which he thought Washington should have extricated him earlier, is inexcusable, in spite of all efforts to excuse it. "You commenced your Presidential career by encouraging and swallowing the grossest adulation, and you traveled America from one end to the other to put yourself in the way of receiving it." [23] This sort of thing could not hurt Washington: it damned Paine.

So much for politics. But, not content with drawing down upon himself the odium of abusing Washington, this light-hearted, quick-tongued iconoclast also set himself to abuse God. The task was even easier, but at the same time a good deal more dangerous. Not that he ever quarreled with God directly.

On the contrary, he always treated the Deity with a tenderness not exempt from patronage. But for those things — whether of religious or social convention — that in his day were chiefly associated with God he had little regard, and he handled them with a fierce sincerity that sent icy shivers down all correct and orthodox backs.

Even here he was not wholly destructive. Indeed he advocated many social reforms that scandalized his own age but are realized, or soon to be realized, in ours. I am not aware that he favored prohibition: he had personal reasons for not doing so. Marriage he respected, and he thought wealth would soon be so harmless that it was not worth bothering with.[24] But he anticipated the abolition of slavery,[25] he anticipated the Society for the Prevention of Cruelty to Animals,[26] he anticipated old age pensions,[27] he anticipated the Shepard-Towner Bill,[28] and he ardently resented the inferior status of women.[29]

Moreover, Paine's religion was constructive enough as regards essentials. He affirmed and reaffirmed, with obvious honesty, his belief in God and his abiding and comforting hope of a future life, though it is interesting to note that his idea of heaven is thoroughly aristocratic: "There is still another description [of men] who are so very insignificant, both in character and conduct, as not to be worth the trouble of damning or saving, or of raising from the dead." [30] Surely these are the very persons whose rights in this world he had been fighting so fiercely to assert. But in general the positive side of "The Age of Reason" and Paine's similar writings is normal, cheerful, and hopeful. There are occasional noble touches, like the saying: "Infidelity does not consist in believing, or in disbelieving; it consists in professing to believe what he does not believe," [31] while no one can question Paine's sincere intent to inspire in his fellow-man "a spirit of trust, confidence, and consolation in his creator." [32] To accomplish this laudable object Paine founded in Paris that pretty dream of an eighteenth-century pedant, the church of Theophilanthropy.

Only he was not a profound thinker. He was shrewd, keen, acute, and his very preoccupation with the surface of things often puts him in the position of modern objective Biblical criticism, without regard to theological subtleties, as Conway justly points out. [33] But the depths of philosophical discussion are utterly beyond him. Above all, he was a rebel: he had no awe, no reverence, and he did like to pull down, cut up, and tear to pieces. When he was eight years old, he made up his mind that "any system of religion that has anything in it that shocks the mind of a child cannot be a true system." [34] When he was nearly sixty, he wrote "The Age of Reason" and knocked the Bible into a cocked hat. The prophets and the disciples, the miracles and the mysteries, the odd adventure of Jonah and the sweet adventure of Ruth, the Virgin and the Magdalen, the Virgin Birth of Christ and the Resurrection, all alike were game for him. He tossed them about and turned them over and worried them like a frolicsome puppy, and when he got through, there was very little left. His object may have been to inculcate "a spirit of trust, confidence, and consolation in the creator"; but what sold his book in huge numbers and made millions read it, as thousands read it still, was something very different and much less edifying.

And though Paine's formal creed was definite and positive enough, there was not an atom of religion in him, no longing, no craving, no aspiration, nothing whatever of the mystic's high emotion and all-absorbing love. Mystery? He abhorred mystery, liked daylight and common sense, and the surface of things. Religion, he expressly explains, cannot have any connection with mystery. As to such matters we know all we need to know, all we ought to know, all we were meant to know. [35]

Which does not imply that the man was not by

nature a believer. Indeed, what perpetually astonishes me is the number of things he believed and his happy faculty of doing it. Perhaps it will be found that the rebel is always a believer, whereas the true conservative is the sceptic, who is afraid to lift his foot, lest he should not know where to set it down. At any rate, Thomas Paine was a believer. He had such a luxuriant faculty of believing that he could afford to throw away an odd belief here and there. Why should anybody mind the loss of a belief or two, when they could be had like cherries for picking from the trees? He believed in man, the honesty of man, the future of man, the rights of man, an endless catalogue, above all he performed the superb logical feat of believing in Thomas Paine. After that, who could call him a sceptic?

The truth is, he had a splendid confidence in human reason. That which, to some of us, seems only an alluring, deceiving will-o'-the-wisp, to be used, since we have nothing better, but never to be trusted, was to Paine a clear light, a sure guide, a sharp, unerring instrument which could be relied on to penetrate to the heart of everything. As bearing on others, this is not quite so certain. They may need a word of caution occasionally: "Alas! nothing is so easy as to deceive one's self." [36] But Thomas

Paine's reason — "My own line of reasoning is to myself as straight and clear as a ray of light," he says in one case [37] and it applies in most cases; for does he not himself tell us that God "has given me a large share of that divine gift?" [38]

You sometimes meet a shrewd, thoughtful, uneducated mechanic who in half an hour will afflict you with reasons, old as the world, but perfectly new and perfectly convincing to him, reasons that smother you like a heap of feathers, as light and as suffocating. Such was Thomas Paine. He had no faintest conception of the huge, involving, shadowing night of ignorance which descends upon the mind that knows something of past and present and honestly and profoundly begins to think. Perhaps he was better off without such conception. The sense of one's own ignorance does little positive good in the world, shatters no idols, rights no wrongs. But it has some pale and negative merits, such as tolerance, patience, humility. It would have done Paine good, if he could have remembered the saying of the great Jefferson, whom he admired, and who was something of a rebel himself: "Error is the stuff of which the web of life is woven and he who lives longest and wisest is only able to weave out the more of it." [39] And ignorance has also the merit of tranquillity. I have "reposed

68

my head on that pillow of ignorance which a benevolent Creator has made so soft for us, knowing how
much we should be forced to use it," says Jefferson
again.[40] Or, in the words with which a poet of to-day
addresses the indulgent, night-enveloped, all-suffusing,
all-enfolding goddess,

> "Grant me thy supreme repose,
> Medicine my vast despairs
> With the calm that never knows,
> And the peace that never cares."

III

REPOSE, humility, and the recognition of ignorance
were not distinguishing features of the character of
Thomas Paine. Still, though he was mainly rebel, he
was not all so: it is interesting to look for the non-
rebel traits in him, however one may be impressed by
their insignificance. Even in his wandering, unsettled, Bohemian career there come gleams of longing
for quiet, tranquillity, domestic peace. When he is in
the thick of European excitement, he writes to Jefferson, "I feel like a bird from its nest, and wishing
most anxiously to return." [41] Of home, of family
surroundings, of the staid continuity of daily routine
he knew little, at least in later years. Perhaps he did
not much care for them. Yet he wrote to a young
lady friend: "Though I appear a sort of wanderer,

the married state has not a sincerer friend than I am. It is the harbor of human life, and is, with respect to the things of this world, what the next world is to this. It is *home;* and that one word conveys more than any other word can express." [42]

Of his relations with women we know little, but enough to be sure that they did not play any considerable part in his life. Although he cared for his mother in her old age, [43] she described him in a letter — possibly not authentic — as "the worst of husbands." [44] His first wife died early. His second left him soon after marriage and it is affirmed that they never had any conjugal relation. After this no woman was closely connected with him except Madame Bonneville, who cared for him in his old age, but without any admissible suggestion of scandal. "His relations with ladies were as chaste as affectionate" is the charming expression of his biographer. [45] I accept the chastity, but doubt whether the affection went very deep. He had no children, but was kind to the children of others and took a moderate interest in them.

As regards men, I find no traces of very near intimacy. Paine of course met all sorts in all places. Some liked him and some detested him, but I do not know that any made a way into his heart. Socially he could be very attractive, when he was in the mood and the company pleased him. He liked to play an occasional game of chess or dominoes, but never cards.[46] To any one who has read his writings it is hardly necessary to say that he had no humor in the sense of irony, no subtle, detached appreciation of the strange, unhinging contrasts of the world. But he had quick, vivid thrusts of wit, his memory was stored with all sorts of apt anecdotes, and he was ready to argue without end. Rickman says of him: "In private company and among friends his conversation had every fascination that anecdote, novelty and truth could give it. In mixed company and among strangers he said little, and was no public speaker."[47]

Of the various æsthetic and intellectual diversions that might afford relief from the strenuous career of rebellion Paine knew little or nothing. It does not appear that he had ever heard of painting or sculpture. He had an ear for music, and liked to take part in a chorus;[48] but his ordinary preoccupations did not leave much place for the finer ecstasies of harmony. One or two passages in his books suggest a certain sensitiveness to the natural world: "Every thing conspired to hush me into a pleasing kind of melancholy — the trees seemed to sleep — and the air hung round me with such unbreathing silence, as if listening to my very thoughts." [49] But these notes are rare, and whatever he learned from Rousseau, it was not his intense passion for the beauty of nature. Nor did he read for the pure delight of it. He had little education in youth and little desire in age to make up for the deficiency. "Indeed," says one who talked with him, "he seems to have a contemptuous opinion not only of books, but of their authors." [50] Even in science, in which he took a constant interest, what attracted him was the purely practical. The fascination of knowing for itself was quite omitted from his composition.

Nor did Paine have any great taste for the enjoyment of life, either in simple amusements or in costly and luxurious ones. His wants were moderate and his way of living frugal, sometimes to the point of privation. For a short period in Paris he had means and kept up a certain establishment.[51] But in the main his surroundings were humble and he knew little of ease or comfort. As he expresses it with his unfailing energy of language, "I have confined myself so much of late, taken so little exercise, and lived so very sparingly, that unless I alter my way of life, it will alter me." [52]

Such a mode of existence did not involve the spending of money, and Paine did not need it, and consequently had no great desire to get it. He constantly proclaimed that his writings were meant to benefit mankind, with no thought of profit, and in spite of their immense circulation, they yielded him practically nothing. When one remembers the sums paid to Byron, Moore, and Scott a few years later, one cannot but admire Paine's disinterestedness, though bare need sometimes drove him to appeals for public assistance that are not entirely prepossessing. Bare need seems to have been all that made him think of money through the greater part of his life. He was free in giving what he had for public and private causes. And never at any time, even in the bitterest attacks on him, was any charge of dishonesty proved or seriously maintained. In his later years it is admitted that he became a trifle parsimonious, but that would appear to have been no more than the dread of a weakening age when the dearest ideal of life has been independence.

Disregard of money is apt to bring disregard of work, and Paine was sometimes accused of indolence, though others insist upon his enormous capacity for labor. J. J. Henry, with whose family he boarded during the Crisis years, remembers him chiefly as eating, sleeping, and dawdling.[53] This is absurd in a man who accomplished so much. The truth is probably that his whole soul toiled by impulse and then rested and relaxed again by impulse, without much thought for order or system, such not being rebel characteristics.

And the same essential disorder of temperament will account for what truth there is in the exaggerated stories of his untidiness. Roosevelt called him a "filthy little atheist," [54] and his hostile biographers, Oldys and Cheetham, give a disgusting picture of his later years. Untended, wandering widowerhood is not always neat, and it may be conceded that Paine's quarters might not have suited a tidy housekeeper. But he was neither filthy, little, nor an atheist. He was of good height and dignified in appearance, with a quick and piercing black eye, [55] and impartial observers describe him in age as careless and indifferent as to his dress, but by no means unpresentable.

The same deductions must be made from the accounts of his drinking. It was a drinking period and Paine was no exception. He himself confessed to Rickman that when he was overcome by discouragement in Paris, he drank heavily, and his drinking was probably not light at other times. His ardent biographer, Conway, whose zeal sometimes overweighs his obvious desire for truth, insists on his idol's sobriety perhaps a little more than it will bear, and I cannot forget the testimony of the printer Chapman at the trial connected with "The Rights of Man," that religion was "a favorite subject with him when intoxicated." [56] But here again the grosser stories are manifestly absurd.

In short, what impresses me most in all these attacks on Paine is their futility. The bitterest enemies, hunting every flaw in a character always exposed to the largest public view, could establish nothing but that he sometimes drank and that he was not clean. These are serious objections to a housemate. No doubt it is good to be clean and sober and conservative and do what your fathers did and shun ideals. But some of us occasionally like to think new thoughts and step out of the beaten track, and we like one who makes us do these things, even if he is a trifle untidy in his person. Here is a man who upset the world and you say he did not brush his clothes. Here is a man who beat and shook conventions, who stirred up dusty and old titles, till he showed their rotten vanity, and you complain because some of the dust got on himself. This is childishness.

IV

For, whatever else Paine was, he was a rebel, delighted in change, delighted in novelty, believed the

75

old order doomed and that he and his like could make the world over and better. "We live to improve, or we live in vain," he wrote, in his swift, incisive fashion,[57] and he meant it. Even his untidiness was in a way a protest against the tiresome formality of life. "Let those dress who need it," he said to a friend.[58] He was interested in innovations of all sorts, theoretical and practical. One of the most useful things he ever did was his invention and designing of iron bridges. He fully shared Franklin's passion for discoveries that would benefit mankind. He tried to contrive the steam engine. He tried to conquer yellow fever. He even added a fine touch to his friend Jefferson's precious gunboats.[59]

He had the rebel's restlessness, could not keep still, did not wish to keep still. When he was sixteen, he began life on a privateer,[60] and from then on he kept moving, moving, always. After the American Revolution he thought he should settle down. But movement possessed him more than ever. He never settled down.

He had the rebel's essential virtue, pugnacity. His Quaker antecedents had instilled into him the love of peace; but that did not prevent a perfect readiness to fight, when fighting was called for. How admirable is his utterance as to this nice Quaker distinction: "I am thus far a Quaker, that I would gladly agree with all the world to lay aside the use of arms, and settle matters by negotiation; but unless the whole will, the matter ends, and I take up my musket and thank heaven he has put it in my power." [61] He did take up his musket, literally, and figured in the revolutionary armies, perhaps with no especial glory, but certainly with no discredit. He had a good, live word for his own physical courage, when addressing Lord Howe, not being given to hiding any of his merits: "I knew the time when I thought that the whistling of a cannon ball would have frightened me almost to death; but I have since tried it, and find that I can stand it with as little discomposure, and, I believe, with a much easier conscience than your lordship." [62] And his moral courage, besides many other proofs, is solidly established by his fine stand for the king's life in the French Convention. No doubt there were other motives mixed with this, as well as mere humanity; but, whatever the motive, it required splendid pluck to vote for clemency in the face of the wolves who were howling for blood.

Also Paine was absolutely sincere. He adopted his principles on what he considered sufficient reasons, and he stuck to them through all abuse and animosity, perhaps with more relish, the greater the abuse. He was not only persistent, he was fiercely obstinate, even in little things, refusing to change what he had written for any one.[63] No threat and no discouragement deterred him. William Duane, who was no conservative, endeavored to dissuade him from religious controversy: "I have fairly told him that he will be deserted by the only party that respects or does not hate him, that all his political writings will be rendered useless, and even his fame destroyed."[64] It was quite unavailing. And the persistency did not falter in the presence of death, though religious partisanship sought to misrepresent this, as with Voltaire and many others. Paine admitted no terror as to the future and no doubt as to the goodness of God. When a benevolent and intrusive old lady in a scarlet cloak visited him in his last illness, insisting that she had a special message from the Almighty urging him to repent, he turned her out, with the apt though petulant comment: "You were not sent with any such impertinent message. ... He would not send such a foolish ugly old woman as you about with his messages. Go away. Go back — shut the door."[65] The old lady went, dissatisfied. He was persistent because he had an immense ardor and enthusiasm, a belief in his cause, in its justice, its nobility, its ultimate triumph, and a determination to live and die serving it.

Not, I think, that Paine had the pure intellectual passion which inspired men like Spinoza or Lucretius and puts them in an altogether different class from Paine's. He did not spend his days and nights in tortured anxiety to arrive at abstract truth. The principles that interested him were those that led to the direct, practical benefit of humanity. He did not concern himself deeply with their philosophical foundations. Though he liked mathematics, he was not an elaborately logical systematic thinker. His intelligence was keen, alert, shrewd, attentive to the surfaces of things and darting rather than delving into the hidden places.

What he did have supremely was the gift of words, and there is no more shining and convenient — and dangerous — weapon in all the rebel's armory. Really the man was an astonishing writer. Critics have been fooled by his ignorance of grammar. Shakespeare was ignorant of grammar, yet some think he could write. Paine was ignorant of everything, though his remarkable memory made him appear to know a great deal. But he certainly was a master of words. They would glow and glitter at his bidding, and fire men's hearts, and turn a small spark into a great flame. They would bite too, and dart and sting and lash, till his victims writhed and

were forced to take refuge in ignoble and usually in
dull retaliation. I think Paine's secret, like Swift's,
lies more in rhythm than in anything else. His dic-
tion is clear and simple and direct; but above all his
phrases snap and crack like whips, with a firm and
vigorous movement that every daily journalist must
envy. How far he understood his own style is a question. He was too busy to study it. That some of the
strange problems connected with words interested
him is evident from his charming remark: "I have
often observed that by lending words for my thoughts
I understand my thoughts the better." [66] That he
appreciated all the terrible dangers of words is unlikely: rebels seldom do appreciate them. But that
he luxuriated in his own verbal power is clear enough.

For he was not a man to miss any of his powers or
let any one else miss them. On the contrary, he enjoyed them thoroughly. He himself tells us that he
was not ambitious: "I never courted either fame or interest." [67] Many other persons make the same boast,
and perhaps in Paine's case it was true, in the larger,
deeper sense. But he had a huge, simple, naïve vanity, which is obvious everywhere, and much increased
as life went on. He liked to be prominent socially,
liked to be "in as elegant style of acquaintance here
as any American that ever came over." [68] He liked

to be prominent politically, thought that Washington "did not perform his part in the Revolution better ... than I did mine, and the one part was as necessary as the other," [69] and he wished others to think so. He enjoyed his literary success, and his candor in asserting it is almost unbelievable: "I have not only contributed to raise a new empire in the world founded on a new system of government, but I have arrived at an eminence in political literature, the most difficult of all lines to succeed and excel in, which aristocracy with all its aids has not been able to reach or to rival." [70]

But even greater than his delight in his own verbal achievements, was his true rebel's delight in destruction. Of course he would have denied this, and maintained that construction was his only true pleasure. Well, construction is pleasant; but it is laborious and uncertain. And destruction is so simple. The enthusiastic biographer betrays the whole secret when he says, "The force of Paine's negations was not broken by any weakness for speculations of his own." [71] It was not, and his infinite, riotous glee in knocking over what antiquity consecrated and ages had revered is so evident as hardly to need confirmation. His gay doings with the Bible were just pure fun. He tells us that when he wrote the first part of "The

Age of Reason," he had no Bible to refresh his mind, and consequently proceeded with some caution; but when he got hold of a copy, he found things so much worse than he thought, that he regretted his former leniency.[72] He made up for it. When he finished, he was able to say: "I have now gone through the Bible, as a man would go through a wood with an axe on his shoulder, and fell trees."[73] Can't you hear his chuckle of real rebel's exultation? The game was so easy to play. As the man says in the French comedy: *"Quel joli métier, et si facile!"* It was such an endless delight to shatter the miracles and overturn the prophets, a cheap and ready amusement that can no longer be enjoyed, since few people to-day take either prophets or miracles seriously enough to be scandalized. But Paine could carry on the merry revel to his heart's content, could smash idols, and grind up crowns, and blast conventions, and turn society topsy-turvy, making one grand climax in the toast which he gave at a public dinner, with gorgeous satisfaction, to "the Revolution of the World."[74]

All which exposure of the weaker side that Paine insisted on exposing so copiously himself should not make us overlook the finer elements in the man's nature. Whatever vanity and self-assertion there may have been in his constant and energetic efforts, and however unpractical and misdirected some may consider them, they were steadily aimed at what he believed to be a lofty object. Through discomfort, through penury, through obloquy he toiled for an ideal. Such a life has a far nobler strain in it than the self-seeking and self-indulgent career of a man like Aaron Burr.

And Paine's work was inspired by the love of humanity. This love is perhaps less manifested in particular instances, though during the French Revolution he labored to save lives rather than to destroy them, and such labor was quite out of fashion. But in the larger sympathy for the poor and downtrodden Paine's merits were real and his accomplishment substantial. His own noble words are absolutely just: "I defend the cause of the poor, of the manufacturers, of the tradesmen, of the farmer, and of all those on whom the real burden of taxes fall — but above all, I defend the cause of humanity." [75] He looked forward, he looked upward, with courage and cheerfulness and hope. He anticipated the large benevolence and benign aspiration of the League of Nations, preached the common interest of all peoples in the pursuit of peaceful progress and democratic advancement,[76] the abolition of war and the cultivation of universal understanding, and it is only just to say that the toast given above to "the Revolution of the World" was transformed a few months later into a similar toast to "the Republic of the World." [77]

So it must be recognized that if Paine, like most rebels, did a considerable amount of harm to mankind, he also did a great amount of good. He taught men to think by his very turbulence, and when you remember how averse they are to that process, he deserves some credit for doing so. He taught them the value of liberty, even if he was not a very sure guide as to the use of it. He taught the worth of a high ideal and the lasting, increasing value of the largest human sympathy. And every American ought to be grateful to him as one of the active founders of the United States of America.

As for the rebels, it must be admitted that, though they are occasionally foul-mouthed and slovenly, and often vain, noisy, and altogether distasteful, they are the power that moves the world. I sometimes wish I had the courage and the character to be a rebel myself.

IV
AARON BURR

CHRONOLOGY

Born, Newark, New Jersey, February 6, 1756.
Graduated from Princeton, 1772.
Took part in Arnold's Expedition to Quebec, 1775.
Left army on account of health, 1779.
Married Theodosia Prevost, July 2, 1782.
Active in law and politics, 1780-1800.
Wife died, 1794.
Elected Vice-President, 1801.
Duel with Hamilton, July 11, 1804.
Tried for treason in Richmond, 1807.
In Europe, 1808-1812.
Theodosia sailed from Charleston, December 30, 1812.
Married Madame Jumel, July 1, 1833.
Died on Staten Island, September 14, 1836.

IV

AARON BURR

I

HE was a man who came into the world to amuse himself, and he early conceived that the richest sources of masculine amusement are the love of women and the domination of men. Perhaps he was right; but it is impossible to deny the justice of John Quincy Adams's grave comment: "Burr's life, take it altogether, was such as in any country of sound morals his friends would be desirous of burying in profound oblivion." [1]

You may regard his career, even more than most, as a series of big and little losses. He was born in 1756. With Jonathan Edwards as his grandfather and the president of Princeton College as his father, he might seem to have inherited an almost suffocating odor of sanctity; but he soon lost it. He lost his parents in early childhood, and he was brought up under what his Edwards uncle regretfully called "a maple-sugar government." [2] As a mere boy, he went with Arnold to Quebec, and followed this with other military distinction; but he lost his health and the favor of Washington and with these the chance of becoming a great soldier. He practised law successfully, but was drawn into politics and showed a wonderful gift for the seamy side of them. He lost the presidency in 1801 by a tie-vote with Jefferson and was thus shifted into that graveyard of greater hopes, the vice-presidency. He lost the governorship of New York, chiefly through the activity of his constant opponent Hamilton. Whereupon he fought and killed Hamilton and by so doing lost the respect of most respectable people. He then schemed to create an empire in the southwest by robbing and possibly ruining his own country. He lost this vast dream hope, and though he was acquitted of treason in a famous trial, he lost what public confidence had been left to him. Money he was always losing, by extravagance, by generosity, by indifference, by windy speculation. He spent four years, from 1808 to 1812, in the most disreputable Bohemian exile in Europe, and at length crept home. Long before, he had lost a charming and beloved wife. He now lost his grandson, whom he worshiped, and the exquisite daughter, who worshiped him. It might seem as if he had nothing left to lose. But he kept on for twenty-five years longer, losing what little trifles life could still take from him. At the very end he married a rich widow and lost first her money and then her affection. And before his death, in 1836, he lost even the use of his limbs. Yet in this crowding, mountainous accumulation of losses, he rarely lost his patience, and never that heaven-bestowed gift of amusing himself.

Through all these busy and tumultuous years Burr loved humanity, all humanity, men, women, and children, and they loved him, especially the women. I have no desire to rake up dusty gossip and forgotten scandal; but to understand such a soul as Burr's, a large analysis of his relations with women is absolutely necessary. Among the various classes of great lovers it is easy to pick out certain types to which Burr did not belong. He had nothing to do with the melancholy, world-weary type, jaded with indiscriminate satiety and restlessly indifferent to anything but the tormenting satisfaction of unappeasable desire, the type which has been so fully and admirably dissected — and illustrated — by Sainte-Beuve. "He experienced the incurable disgust for all things which is peculiar to those who have abused the sources of life," [3] would be ludicrously inept as a description of Burr.

Nor was he a longing, absorbed, soul-devouring, romantic lover. I do not believe he ever lost a night's sleep or a day's work in vainly dreaming of a woman. The supreme line which expresses such a state of mind,

" I was not, save it were a thought of thee,"
would have been meaningless to him, and his
daughter brands the romantic as something "which,
thanks to my father on earth, I am long past." [4]

Again, though here some critics would differ, I am
convinced that Burr did not belong to the group
of the bitter, cynical lovers, the Lovelace class, who
pursue from vanity and conquer with contempt,
blighting virtue and innocence merely to prove that
they have no existence. Burr had a naïve vanity
which led him to take a considerable satisfaction
in his popularity with women. But it seems solidly
proved that he did not boast of individual triumphs;
and, while we can never place implicit trust in the
many verbal statements that are attributed to him, I
believe that in a general way and with reasonable
allowances, there was truth, at least of intention, in
the remark: "Nor did I ever do, or say, or write
anything which threw a cloud over a woman's
name." [5]

In short, however indiscriminate and disreputable
were Burr's amours, there seems to have been nothing
perverse or abnormal about them. His pleasure in his
relations with women was mainly part of the entertainment he derived at all times from the society of
his fellow human beings. The sting of sex added a

peculiar and enchanting piquancy; but the entertainment was general and inexhaustible. He liked people, liked to be with them, and to watch them, and to talk to them. His manner was always dignified and not obtrusively or aggressively sympathetic. His admirers compared his social ease as well as his morals with those of Chesterfield, and he liked to have them do so. But he was infinitely more genuine than Chesterfield, simpler and far more lovable. In many respects he recalls that creature of vast and abounding humanity, the elder Dumas. He had a passion for a sort of superficial mystery, as a child has. But in fact he was candid. If he said different things at different times, it was because he felt different things. And at all times he entered into the lives of others, laughed with them, played with them, wept with them: "You, who can so well and so singularly bring home to yourself the feelings of others, and adopt them when they are quite strange to you," said his daughter, admirably.⁶ Above all, he had the delightful gift of making others' amusement his own, and his is the charming and perfectly human phrase, "It is a luxury to see people happy."

His attraction for grown men was undeniable and was exercised all over the world. He made innumerable devoted friends of all sorts, friends who were loyal to him and faced great sacrifices for him. From the strange vicissitudes of his life, and, alas, from his own fundamental selfishness, he lost most of them; but he found it incredibly easy to make others. "Every variety of man," says Mr. Oliver, "rich and poor, old and young, honest citizen or reckless outlaw, every casual acquaintance and simple wayfarer, is won with the same magic. They like him because they believe that he likes them and understands them, which there is little doubt he did."[7] This may be somewhat exaggerated and requires correction by Mr. Lodge's harsh remark that Burr possessed "what women and young men call 'fascination.'"[8] But of the two I think Mr. Oliver is nearer the truth.

And if Burr attracted men, it is certain that he was even more attractive to children, and again because he evidently loved them. The truth is that, like Dumas, he was in many respects a child himself, though sometimes a rather sophisticated one; and he was always ready to leave the great matters of the world to romp and frolic with congenial playmates. "As for children," says Mr. Oliver again, "they followed him as if he had been the Pied Piper of Hamelin."[9] Burr's letters and journals are full of bits showing this pure and kindly sympathy with the childish heart. How pretty is his account of the little German girl, six years old, with the guitar, whom he snubs: "To be sure, I did give her a gooden groshen, which was probably much more than she expected; but I was unkind. One minute after I was sorry, and sent for her, but she was not to be found; and I have been all day looking out for her in vain." [10]

This tender regard for children is everywhere obvious in Burr's own domestic affairs. His daughter Theodosia was one of the great delights and interests of his life. He devoted much care and thought to her education and sought to give her an intellectual training far different from what fell to most of the women of her time. She did him credit in every way; for she was admired and beloved, not only for her beauty, but for her character, by all who came into contact with her. Even those, like Blennerhassett, who had suffered by her father's vagaries, did not allow their grudge against him to affect their adoration for her. [11] Burr's letters to her show him at his best and are full of practical and moral advice most excellent in quality, if a little surprising from such a source. He prides himself upon his influence over her, which was undoubtedly great; but she was the stronger nature and it is probable that she had even more influence over him. When she married the wealthy South Carolinian Joseph Allston, her only son, Burr's namesake, became almost as much an object of affection and solicitude as the mother was.

If Burr was fond of his daughter, it was partly because she resembled her mother, and as a husband he is no less attractive than as a father. The marriage was one of affection. The elder Theodosia was older than her husband, and was neither rich nor strikingly handsome. Burr was attached to her because he appreciated the singular grace, dignity, and elevation of her character and mind, and all his life he spoke with reverence of her charm and of the value of her influence upon him. Yet it is notable that her loss, when he was well under forty, seems to have made no very profound impression, and still more notable is the difference in tone between her letters and his. His are affectionate, considerate, thoughtful, helpful. Hers have a rare and high intensity of passion which he never knew. She says in simple, pregnant words of one of his: "How is it possible you had nothing more to write? I know the head may be exhausted, but I was in hopes the heart never could." [12]

In fact, Burr's love for his wife was only part of his love for all her sex. And it must at once be recognized that this love did not stop short of unlimited licentiousness. As a subject for the psychoanalysts Burr must be singularly fruitful. Even the plain old-fashioned psychologist must regard him with a considerable amount of interest. His biographers proclaim a touching confidence in his marital fidelity. As Ariosto says of his heroine in a similar connection: "It may be true, but it is extremely improbable." Parton, endeavoring to contradict Davis, who would have saved his hero's political character at the expense of his moral, even insists that Burr was virtuous before his marriage. But Parton had not seen the unedited version of Burr's Journal. Any one who has read that ingenuous document, even though it deals with later life, does not find it difficult to believe the stories as to Jacataqua, the Indian girl, on the march to Quebec, as to Margaret Moncrieffe, or any other stories. It is not necessary or possible to emphasize this utterly dissolute side of Burr's character further than to point out that he seems to have had no idea of moral scruple in such matters. Indeed, his entire absence of compunction gives his dealings a singularly demoralizing charm, which is suggestive of Sterne; and I wish I could embellish these decorous pages with the gay adventure of the fair Madame D. in the crowded inn at Rotterdam,[13] an adventure which seems to have danced airily right out of the last chapter of "A Sentimental Journey."

The curious thing is that his wild illicit relations

did not, as is so often the case, destroy or diminish Burr's perfectly innocent pleasure in the society of virtuous persons of the other sex. In all his eighty years he never made the ghastly discovery that a pretty woman can be a bore. He would meet a charming stranger, chat and flirt with her for an hour, kiss her hand respectfully, sigh over her departure, forget her, and be ready for the next. He would at once have acknowledged the significance of the words of Pepys: "Which is a strange slavery that I stand in to beauty, that I value nothing near it." [14] All fashions and all types suited him. The plump, the thin, the dark, the fair, the gay, the grave, even the plain, so they were merry, or witty, or tender, or tantalizing — all alike had a fascination for him.

And as he found all women attractive, so they responded with an almost unanimous cordiality. One cannot say what the secret was; one seldom can in these cases. He was not strikingly handsome, though his courtly and gracious manners, his sympathetic voice, and his intense, quick eyes may have helped. The solution was just the plain old one of Victor Hugo's verses:

> "Comment, disaient ils,
> Enchanter les belles
> Sans philtres subtils?
> Aimer, disaient elles."

Burr liked women, and women liked him: that was all there was to it. The gay loved him to laugh with him, the pious to reform him, both with the same ardor, though not with the same success. When he met a siren, he asked kisses, when he visited a convent, he asked prayers.[15] Prayers and kisses alike were accorded with celerity and accepted with gratitude.

What Burr's fundamental opinion of women was, is not easy to ascertain. He was not a brooding analyst of himself or of others, and no doubt he preferred to enjoy rather than to explain. He often puts himself forward as the defender of their intelligence and he remonstrated against the shallow education which was all that most women of that day received. At the same time, like many wide lovers, he does not seem to have been generally inclined to submit the practical conduct of his life to their influence, and I suspect that in the depths of his heart he regarded them as the most amusing toys in an amusing world. When one of them asked him "But, Colonel, have ladies no sense then?" his gentle answer was, "*All* sense, madame; yet is it better to talk sweet little nothings to them." [16]

Whatever he thought of them, they played a huge part in his life. If we can believe Parton —

alas, so often we cannot — his very last faintly whispered dying word was "Madame." [17] And after his poverty-stricken death the monument which his careless and indifferent executors had neglected to place over his grave was set up in the anonymity of night by the orders of a woman who had loved him. [18]

II

THUS we have established that Burr was a man who adored women. If it be thought that this is incompatible with a life of strenuous activity and at least attempted achievement, we should remember Mirabeau, who adored women, but snatched time from them to make over his country, and Mohammed, who adored women, but snatched time from them to make over the world. I have dealt thus largely, in beginning, with the element of feminine amusement in Burr's life, because I believe that, though he owed his place in American history to far other pursuits, the key of amusement is just as important in interpreting these as in understanding his lighter hours. The efforts of practical life, and he was capable of mighty ones, were to him, not stages in an ideal structure of vast achievement, but mere diversions, like the kiss of a girl, and hardly more engaging.

Nevertheless, he did great things, and was closely

entangled in far greater. In his youth the Revolution made him think that the highest of human amusements would be to be a soldier, and he bade fair to be a brave, discreet, far-seeing, and successful one. He made his little, frail body iron, by stern temperance, discipline, and self-control.[19] Indeed, he was always temperate in food and drink. He made his soldiers work, fight, and love him. I think perhaps the greatest amusement, and certainly the noblest, of his life was bearing the body of his dead general Montgomery off the field, in the blinding snow, with the British guns threatening to bring him down at every moment. But over-exertion and health tried beyond all reason cut off this career too soon.

Then there was law, a fascinating, stimulating, absorbing amusement. And there was work in it, no doubt, enormous work. But the work might be made amusing also, especially when it led to a brilliant triumph. Even Burr's admirers do not insist that he was a profound or philosophical lawyer. His respect for the profession is indicated in his cynical comment on law as "whatever is boldly asserted and plausibly maintained." [20] But he worked hard, his energy and his industry were as intelligently directed as they were untiring, and it is remarkable that law is the one phase of his career in which he did not lose. It is even said that he never lost a case in which he was engaged alone.[21] Well would it have been for him, had he stuck to law altogether, and not abandoned it for other forms of amusement, perhaps no more diverting and at any rate less profitable.

Unfortunately the fascination of politics, so baneful to the lawyer in a democratic government, soon drew him into its snare. For a certain kind of political career Burr was admirably fitted. He was not troubled with an excess of moral scruple, and if the phrase, "Great souls care little for small morals," [22] was not correctly attributed to him, it might have been. He was an able organizer, or at any rate manipulator. And he was a cunning and a mighty adept in the art of moulding and kneading the souls of men. What his power in this way was may be well indicated by his singular and impressive account of what on one occasion happened to himself. "From any man, save one, if I cannot vanquish, I can escape. In the hands of that one, I am just what Theodosia is in mine. This was perceived after the first two hours; and seeing no retreat, nor anything better to be done, I surrendered, tame and unresisting, to be disarmed, stripped, hacked, hewed, dissected, skinned, turned inside out, at the will and mercy of the operator." [23] The treatment he experienced in this case seems to be about what he applied at different times to scores of others.

Yet the gifts were unavailing. It would be impossible to analyze here the complex tangle of Burr's political life. Suffice it to say that after fifteen years of it he came out in 1805 completely and generally discredited and distrusted by all parties alike. In 1801 he lost the presidency by the tie with Jefferson. In 1804 he was defeated in the contest for the New York governorship, then almost as great an office as the presidency. Through all these political struggles the chief obstacle to Burr's success was the bitter and increasing antagonism of Hamilton, founded partly on personal jealousy but mainly on a deep and well-grounded belief in Burr's dangerous and unscrupulous ambition. In the spring of 1804 the rivalry between the two grew so fierce that Burr determined to end it by mortal combat, for which Hamilton himself admitted that he had given excuse;[24] and Hamilton's most brilliant biographer says of Burr's challenge: "Few gentlemen have ever sent a friend with a message upon more substantial provocation."[25] The duel took place on the eleventh of July, and was conducted properly according to the etiquette of such affairs. Burr fired to kill and inflicted a mortal wound. Probably Hamilton discharged his pistol with a convulsive pressure, as he was struck; but the bullet flew far wide of his adversary. On that July morning on the Heights of Weehawken Burr tossed his future in the air and shot it to pieces like a glass pigeon, just from a whim of spite, or was it really from a notion of honor? Either way, it was thoroughly characteristic of the man.

Only a very brief time after the duel was required to show Burr that, however it might be judged as a matter of morals, it was ruinous as a matter of policy. A howl of horror rose from the Federalists and from nearly all decent people; and Burr was obliged practically to seclude himself for a time. Indeed, his situation was almost desperate, and he knew it was, and had intense, if brief, periods of dejection. Yet in these months of wandering and distress his letters to Theodosia show no regret, but constantly his singular power of amusing himself, and I am not aware of any sign of remorse for Hamilton's death, unless the remark in later years, "If I had read Sterne more and Voltaire less, I should have known that the world was wide enough for Hamilton and me." [26]

By the autumn of 1804, however, things had quieted down sufficiently for Burr to resume his vice-presidential place in the Senate. Many people dreaded and avoided him, but no one cared to attack him; and his extraordinary fascination was as widely exerted as ever. He presided with dignity and impartiality at the impeachment of Judge Chase, and on the second of March, 1805, he delivered a farewell address. It was a noble, a dignified, a perfectly appropriate speech and contained the striking and possibly prophetic words so often quoted: "If the Constitution be destined ever to perish by the sacrilegious hands of the demagogue or the usurper, which God avert, its expiring agonies will be witnessed on this floor." [27] I can quite well imagine Dumas making just such a speech, with entire solemnity and real feeling. But the sentence that impresses me most is one that would not have been preserved to us except for the record of John Quincy Adams, who watched the whole ceremony with profound attention. Burr enjoins upon Senators the importance of adhering to their regular rules of order; for, he says, "on full investigation it will be discovered that there is scarce a departure from order but leads to or is indissolubly connected with a departure from morality." [28] Think of these words, from Aaron Burr, who cared just as much for morality as he did for order! And is it not a delightful bit of humor that the passage should have been handed down by Adams, poor, gaunt-souled John Quincy Adams, eaten up by conscience, who had

never known an hour of amusement in his whole life?
Adams and Burr!

Within two years this ardent eulogist of order and
morality was busily conspiring against the peace, if
not the existence, of his country, whose dying agonies
he was content to leave for exhibition on the floor of
the Senate, or anywhere else. The snarl of efforts and
accusations and individualities and passions involved
in the Burr Conspiracy is too intricate to be elucidated in a brief portrait, if it can be elucidated at all.
Henry Adams's narrative shows Burr directly aiming
to break up the Union.[29] Dr. McCaleb would have us
believe that this was all a pretense, that the enthusiastic loyalty of the West would have made such an
attempt ludicrous, and that Burr's designs were directed only against Spain, with the whole West in entire sympathy.[30] Even the plain facts are exceedingly difficult to get at. But it is certain that during
1805 and 1806 Burr studied the western country
carefully, attached to himself a considerable number
of adherents, conspicuous among whom were the de-
luding Wilkinson and the deluded Blennerhassett, and
even, at any rate as a matter of friendship, Andrew
Jackson and Henry Clay, provided himself with a
decent excuse in the purchase of a tract of land for
ostensible settlement, and in the autumn of 1806 set

out with a handful of followers to descend the Mississippi toward New Orleans, and accomplish —
something; what, we shall never know. Twice he was
hindered on his way by the authorities, was tried and
triumphantly acquitted. But at last the government
was so thoroughly aroused that he found it expedient
to leave his followers and attempt to make his escape.
The attempt failed, and he was arrested and taken
to Richmond to be tried for treason.

Through all this parti-colored Odyssey what Burr
really planned to accomplish still remains obscure.
Probably it was obscure even to himself. I have
already pointed out that he had a certain childlike love
of mystery, which showed in a taste for enveloping
even simple matters in cipher. His celebrated cipher
letter to Wilkinson has a flavor of comic opera, though
it deals with life and death. In short, he was a
conspirator, as Mr. Lodge suggests,[31] rather than a
statesman, and great undertakings are not built on
conspiracy. From all the conflicting and concurring
pieces of evidence we gather that he dreamed of
a cloudy empire, founded on the ruins of Spanish
power in the Southwest, an empire that should give
modern progress and civilization to those oppressed
people and incidentally a glittering throne to himself, to be transmitted by inheritance to his daughter.

If this seems utterly fantastic, we must remember that Napoleon was then at the top of his success, with no shadow of approaching overthrow, and that scores of military adventurers like Burr were stimulated by his example. What moves me more than all the elaborate legal testimony is one brief phrase of Theodosia's, which shows the hopes and dreams and schemes the two had talked over together. Writing later to her father in Europe, she says of difficulties affecting Mexico: "It is generally believed that we shall have trouble very soon. Thank God I am not near my subjects; all my care and real tenderness might be forgotten in the strife."[32] It is these little touches that betray the secrets of the heart.

What chiefly wrecked Burr's Mexican scheme was the lack of money. He begged, he borrowed, he inveigled and plundered rich fools like Blennerhassett, he had the delightful audacity to ask the Spanish government for money to destroy itself. All was to no purpose. What he got was pitiful, and even that slipped through his fingers. Money always slipped through his fingers: it was the tragedy of his life, except that he made it a comedy. He was often accused of dishonesty, and as he refused to justify himself — he never would justify himself — the accusation stuck. Perhaps he deserved it, indirectly at any rate.

But the chief trouble was an utter incapacity for dealing with money at all. He had a good gift at earning. He had an enormous gift at spending. He liked to spend for himself. He liked to spend for others, regardlessly, indiscriminately. Any beggar could fool him. "I never buy a bit of furniture or take the smallest trip without being duped and plundered; and, when it is past, I console myself with the experience I have gained, and the full assurance that it is the very last time; and this has gone on pretty much the same way near forty years."[33] He liked speculation of all sorts, liked to make cloud fortunes, and squander them generously and recklessly. Was there ever a prettier picture of milkmaid's happiness than this? "Now if I can get a passport to Bremen and Amsterdam," he writes to his daughter at a later period, "I will send you a million of francs within six months; but one half of it must be laid out in pretty things. Oh! what beautiful things I will send you. . . . Home at ten, and have been casting up my millions and spending it. Lord, how many people I have made happy."[34]

So, in casting up his millions and spending them and making people happy and inventing huge visionary amusement, he landed himself in Richmond and was being tried for his life. The trial was an immense spectacle; but it was a farce. Everybody, from the chief justice to the slightest witness and the prisoner himself, seemed to be thinking of something besides his guilt or innocence. All the same, the ignominy of it set the stamp upon his terrible failure. He had failed in politics, he had failed in the conception of empire, simply because he was not big enough, because he did not take life or death or other men or his own ambition seriously enough. Perhaps, after all, he was quite as happy. He had the temperament of happiness. Even in destruction and disaster there were elements of amusement, if you knew how to look for them. Theodosia writes of her stay in Richmond during the trial: "Indeed, my father, so far from accepting of sympathy, has continually animated all around him. . . . Since my residence here, of which some days and a night were passed in the penitentiary, our little family circle has been a scene of uninterrupted gayety." [35]

And this was the man who so narrowly missed being president of the United States. We do not know what sort of a president he would have been; but we do know something of what, as vice-president, he was. And there is always that sentence in the farewell to the Senate: "On full investigation it will be discovered that there is scarce a departure from order but leads to or is indissolubly connected with a departure from morality." A grave sentence, an admirable sentence; but, coming from those lips, it too much recalls the old adage about Satan reproving sin.

O Aaron Burr, O Aaron Burr, you amused yourself and you were the cause of endless amusement — and misery — in others.

III

AFTER being formally acquitted of treason and even of misdemeanor, Burr sailed for Europe in 1808, partly because his enemies and his creditors made America unpleasant and partly in the shadowy hope of furthering his Mexican schemes. He was received at first fairly well in England and Scotland and had agreeable social relations. But the government soon became suspicious of him, and he was driven into a forlorn exile over the northern part of the continent. The record of his four years' wandering is contained in his singular Journal. And it ought to be a record of despair. Not only had he left great hope behind him, not only had the wealth and glory and power he had dreamed of utterly faded away, while all he loved was separated from him by a thousand leagues of barren sea. But he was beset with every sort of petty trial and discomfort. He knocked in vain at the portals of

the great, or shivered in their antechambers and endured the insults of their lackeys, soliciting aid or
favor or even tolerance. He had spells of sickness, of
sheer physical exhaustion, with nobody to tend him.
He was forced to tramp the streets when "my legs refused their office; my knees trembled, and my head
became dizzy, so that I was each moment in danger
of falling and being run over." [36]   He endured discomforts of cold, discomforts of heat, discomforts of
wet and filth and vermin. He was utterly, wretchedly
poor, so that he was often near his last penny, forced
to borrow of servants and casual acquaintance,
forced to sell the petty and treasured remembrances
of brighter days. He writes to Theodosia: "So, after
turning it over, and looking at it, and opening it,
and putting it to my ear like a baby, and kissing it,
and begging you a thousand pardons out loud, your
dear, little beautiful watch was — was sold." [37]

Well, in spite of this hideous accumulation of great
and little miseries — the little so often harder to endure — the record is not one of despair at all. There
are moments of depression, perhaps more intense for
their rarity, but in the main there is a sunny, infec-
tious cheerfulness, which is quite irresistible. And
this cheerfulness is not stoical, is not a matter of discipline and theory. No doubt Burr's theory supported

his practice; but the practice was constitutional and did not require any theory whatever. There is no regret for the past, hardly even a thought of it. There is occasional preoccupation with the future, but not often to the point of anxiety. There is always recognition of the golden sufficiency of the present, and the wisdom of making the most of it by keeping one's thoughts outside of one's self.

And note that the ordinary greater spiritual consolations and resources are not so much what Burr depends upon. He was never an absorbed or arduous thinker, and he did not divert himself with the problems of philosophy. He read widely, but at this time mainly current matter of the day. He took little interest in art, though his quick susceptibility responded to it for the moment. He says that he could spend a month looking at paintings,[38] but I do not observe that he often spends an hour, and one of the few that he describes in detail is the likeness of a lady in decided undress.[39] When he hears a concert, he is more interested in the audience than in the music;[40] and the natural world, also, is little more than a background for humanity. As to religion, it is hardly to be supposed that he looked to it for comfort. In his youth he threw off inherited Calvinism once for all.[41] In his age he spoke of the Bible with respect,[42] but

III

nothing suggests a daily perusal. He manifested a good deal of confidence that he would be vindicated in heaven from the few sins which he had not committed on earth and from which he had been too proud or too lazy to vindicate himself.[43] In general, his attitude is that of a polite acquaintance with God, such as he maintained with all gentlemen, but of no particular intimacy. I don't know what can better sum up his religion than his delightful remark: "I think that God is a great deal better than people suppose."[44]

But he did not need these greater and more remote means of spiritual support, because the mere casual amusement of every day and hour was enough. He lived on the surface of his own soul, and the bright, varied, shifting, scintillating surface of life afforded him inexhaustible diversion. When he was cold and half-sick and poverty-stricken indoors, he could go to a theatre on the boulevards and laugh and cry like a forgetful child. He could walk in the fields on a sunny morning and meet a gay company of peasants and chat with them and take part in their simple sports and make them think he was as gentle and innocent as they were — and in a sense he was. Or, if he had to take a long dark ride in a crowded coach, with the wind chilling and the rain beating, he could wrap himself in his cloak, and snuggle up for warmth against the stout farmer beside him, and smile, and fall asleep.

And the inward cheerfulness was reflected in an outward kindness and courtesy, which won hearts even if it could not keep heads. He was ready to receive favors, and when he could, to return them, to give money, when he had it, and to give smiles, which he always had. His hope was no greater than his benevolence, which was extraordinary, considering his evanescent means; often no doubt indiscreet and foolish, but immensely attractive. Could there be anything prettier than the story of the halfpence? "Have left in cash two halfpence, which is much better than *one* penny, because they jingle, and thus one may refresh one's self with the music." [45] Yet a little later he finds himself penniless, "for I had given my two half-pence to Gonin's little girl." [46]

Then there are the women, women innumerable, unfailing, and amusing always. There is that strange multiplicity of indiscriminate street adventures, which are saved from utter sordidness only by the grace and sunshine of his spirit. On a higher level there are such entanglements as that with Madame de Reizenstein, and the escape from her, described with such picturesque vividness: "Felicitate me, my dear, on my escape from the most critical danger of

my life. . . . I do really believe that de Reizenstein is a
sorceress. Indeed, I have no doubt of it; and, if I were
president of the Secret Tribunal, she should be burned
alive to-morrow. Another interview, and I might
have been lost; my hopes and projects blasted and
abandoned. The horror of this last of catastrophes
struck me so forcibly, and the danger was so imminent, that at eight o'clock I ordered posthorses; gave
a crown extra to the postillion to drive like the devil,
and lo! here I am in a warm room, near a neat, good
bed, safely locked within the walls of Erfurth, re-
joicing and repining." [47] But with high and low,
rich and poor, virtuous and sordid, there is the same
cordiality, the same gayety, the same lavish waste of
limited means, and the same easy oblivion. "Four
francs for a prostitute and brandy; two for benevolence." [48] There you have Aaron Burr—at fifty-five.

The Journal which contains all these edifying bits
is a curious production. Professor Channing calls it
"the most disgraceful journal in existence." [49] To
lovers of Pepys this must seem rather strong. At the
same time, though Pepys is more luxuriant in detail,
Burr distinctly excels in the complete absence of that
conscience which was always teasing and towsling and
tormenting poor Pepys, after his indecorous excesses.
In other respects the diaries oddly resemble each

114

other. Both are broken, frank, direct, almost incoherent notes of the day's intimate experiences, without any attempt at literary finish, Burr indeed taking pains to emphasize that he is merely making jotted memoranda for future use. Both show that singular and unexpected yet intensely human disposition, to disguise misdoing under a veil of polyglot shyness, and in both the use of foreign languages is as careless as it is chaotic. Only, a slight study of Burr is sufficient to convince one of the supreme genius of Pepys in the instinctive analysis of his own soul.

The strangest, most inexplicable thing about Burr's Journal is that it was explicitly and solely intended for Theodosia's reading. Biographers have tried to make out that she was to have an expurgated duplicate, but the evidence of the diary itself tends to disprove this assertion.[50] The only possible way to explain the difficulty is to remember Burr's extraordinary, childlike, Dumas-like candor, and the peculiar independence of Theodosia's bringing up; but even so, the problem is troublesome enough. At any rate, the existence of the Journal shows what an immense place the daughter occupied in her father's thought; and it serves to remind us that during these terrible European years he had at least the vision of her and of an old age passed in her company. What

that company was, what an influence her intense
fragility and beautiful, noble courage had on a nature
so difficult to influence is obvious everywhere in the
many letters she wrote him, letters which show a
character subtler, stronger, more framed to fill a
great place in the world than his. And yet, as so often
happens, the very strength of the higher nature
showed itself in an adoration of the lower which is
almost overwhelming in its passionate ardor: "Often,
after reflecting on this subject, you appear to me so
superior, so elevated above all other men; I contem-
plate you with such a strange mixture of humility,
admiration, reverence, love, and pride, that very little
superstition would be necessary to make me worship you as a superior being; such enthusiasm does
your character excite in me." [51] The eternal tragedy of deluded affection has no more pathetic victims than Margaret Arnold and Theodosia Burr, and
with what scorn they would both have resented the
word!

So, when Burr, in 1812, finally succeeded in slink-
ing home from Europe, he had at least this affection
and that of his grandchild to look forward to. Then
the hope was blighted by sudden and overwhelming
disaster. A few weeks after Burr landed in New
York his grandchild died. This blow was serious

enough: it completely prostrated Theodosia. But at least she and her father could be together. On the last day but one of 1812 she sailed from Charleston for New York, and was never heard of again.

It seemed as if life could hold no more wretchedness. Even Burr's serenity was shaken for a time, and he admitted in despair that he "felt severed from the human race." [52] Yet the wonderful elasticity of that wonderful spirit brought him up again, and for twenty-five years he lived on in New York, presumably very much the life that he had lived before. He was shunned by society and coldly regarded by other members of his profession; yet he practised law with the same old vital vigor and with notable success. His immense physical activity continued almost to the end; and, in the main, the cheerfulness, the kindly interest in people about him, the endless faculty of finding and imparting amusement persisted, unimpaired. Also, his wild and unrestrained dealings with money increased, if possible. He was always hopelessly in debt. He had found out long before that "this 'giving' is a very unprofitable business, and I have twenty times determined to quit it, yet am perpetually 'seduced into the perpetration of it.' " [53] He gave right and left, whenever he had anything to give, without discrimination and without regret.

And when he was seventy-seven, he married. The affair was as picturesque as everything else about him. The lady, Madame Jumel, who was rich and by no means young, had some natural hesitation. Burr laughingly told her that he would come on a certain day with a clergyman, prepared for business. The day came, and Burr, and the clergyman, the same who had married him to Theodosia fifty years before. The lady yielded and the marriage took place. But, alas, the conjugal felicity lasted little longer than the wooing, and the wife soon left the husband to his old, congenial, discreditable solitude.

There is little more to the strange story: paralysis shattering the body, but not great or grave enough to perturb the dauntless spirit, and the self-forgetful care of a woman who was willing to face slander and obloquy to ease the last days of her father's old friend. On the fourteenth of September, 1836, Aaron Burr died.

Apparently he had little fear of death, by steel, or bullet, or disease. When a lady was complaining to him that some misery would kill her, he said, "Well, die then, madame: we must all die; but, bless me, die game." [54] He died game. When he was in Paris, he thought he had been poisoned, and remembered the fate of a friend, who "having taken a dose of medicine, some time after drank a glass of cold water, and in an hour was dead. It seemed to me that I was about to follow his example; and, being in good company, and feeling no pain, there could not be a more charming occasion for an exit. I became very gay, and F. said I was never *si aimable.*" [55] In his last illness a reverend gentleman asked him as to his hope of salvation through Christ. He replied that "on that subject he was coy." [56] Is not the phrase admirably characteristic of the man, so that you feel sure you have his very words? And is it not delicious? He replied that on that subject he was coy. Should n't you think he might have been? He had murdered his rival, conspired against his country, deserted his followers, robbed his friends, made a plaything of female virtue; and really one shudders to think where he must have gone to. Yet he had done it all in the most amiable spirit. "Revenge, you know," he says, "is not in my nature." [57] And he referred casually in company to his great adversary as "my friend Hamilton, whom I shot." [58] Wherever he went, it is difficult to think of him as not enjoying himself, and one is constantly reminded of the charming remark of Fowler in "The Witty Fair One," when he believes he is in hell: "If I be dead, I am in a world very like the other. I will get myself a female spirit to converse withal, and kiss, and be merry, and imagine myself alive again."

Once more I recur to that inimitable sentence in the Senate speech: "On full investigation it will be discovered that there is scarce a departure from order but leads to or is indissolubly connected with a departure from morality." [59] It is said that Senators wept. I imagine the angels wept also. Fortunately not even the tears of angels can ever blot out that sentence.

JOHN RANDOLPH OF ROANOKE

CHRONOLOGY

Born, Cawsons, Virginia, June 2, 1773.
For a short time at Princeton and at Columbia Colleges.
Elected to Congress, 1799.
Attacked Yazoo claim, 1805.
Separated from Jefferson and party, 1806.
Fought Henry Clay, April 8, 1826.
Mission to Russia, 1830.
Died, Philadelphia, May 24, 1833.

V

JOHN RANDOLPH OF ROANOKE

I

OF all this group of damaged souls John Randolph of Roanoke was in some respects the noblest; and for that very reason he seems the most pitifully and fatally damaged. A Virginian biographer calls him "the most remarkable character that this country has ever produced."[1] Professor Channing, more moderately, speaks of him as "one of the half dozen greatest men of his time."[2] Even the critical Henry Adams, who bared Randolph's faults so unmercifully, describes him in his earlier and better days as "a sort of Virginian Saint Michael, almost terrible in his contempt for what seemed to him base or untrue."[3] Yet the admirable endowments that earned this praise were blighted by defects of temper and nerves which made the man's influence for good largely null.

Randolph was born in 1773. He began his public life when little more than a boy, and from that time till his death at sixty he was always fighting something. He opposed Adams the father in 1800, he opposed Adams the son in 1825. Between these two, both in the House and during his brief term in the Senate, he opposed all parties, all movements, and pretty much all men. In his long political career there were two conspicuous attempts at positive achievement: in 1805 he was manager of the Chase impeachment trial, which failed; in 1829 he accepted a special mission to Russia, remained there a few weeks, and received a year's salary.[4] But in the main he was a furious negative, nothing more. His private life is summed up by saying that he was always opposed to his own best interests. It is a striking thing that this man, whose soul was all oddity, should have grown up and passed his best years on an estate called Bizarre. What strange tricks Fate does play with us!

A true portrait of Randolph must, alas, be in great part occupied with eccentricities and defects. But it is necessary to assert and emphasize the noble qualities which might have given him lasting glory, if he had not thrown them away. He had courage, he had magnificent, exhaustless energy and initiative, he had sincerity, he had honesty. The little adventure in Russia might seem to contradict this, though Senator Bruce, in his excellent biography of Randolph, energetically defends his conduct in the matter.[5] In his last years financial pressure and thrift inclined Randolph to be careful of the dollars. But during his whole life he branded and exposed political corruption and there is no reason to think that he would have succumbed to it. His patriotism was not all declamation, but was founded on a genuine ardor and effort for the welfare of his country.

His constructive statesmanship was never really tested and possibly did not exist. But he had a profound insight into the workings of American democracy, shown in many sayings like this: "As to the body of the people, their intentions are always good, *since it can never be their interest to do wrong*," [6] and in his urgent wish that the heads of cabinet departments might be present in Congress.[7]

He had a singular power of leading and controlling men. To be sure, this was accomplished more by fear than by love. He bullied his followers, quite as much as he charmed them. It would be hard to say whether his Virginian constituents more worshiped or detested him; and the House regarded him alternately with astonishment, dismay, delight, and disgust.

This result was of course mainly obtained by his oratory. Take him all in all, he seems to have been the most startling and effective, if not the most edifying and influential speaker that American politics have known. His speeches had not weight, they had not substance. There was none of the solid massing of argument to a logical conclusion that distinguishes the great political thinkers who have swayed the world. Indeed, as years went by, Randolph's speaking drifted off into a flood of incoherent irrelevance, which he himself repeatedly recognized and apologized for. He could not stick to the subject, did not try to, did not wish to. But even this irrelevant natural ease seems to have added to the charm. There was a swift, keen penetration, a vivid lighting up of dark corners in motives and in souls, a terrible, intense emphasis on things that the cautious let alone, which made men listen, made them think, made them sometimes, perhaps, go away and live differently, even if the difference consisted in being as unlike as possible to the strange creature who had searched their hearts. "The interest of Randolph's speeches," said Josiah Quincy, "was that he simply exposed his intellect and let you see it at work."[8] Now some orators dread such exposure, and some have not the intellect to expose.

With these gifts and powers it is profoundly interesting to find out why Randolph accomplished so little. It was not for lack of ambition. He did indeed repeatedly disclaim the desire for office: he knew enough of himself to appreciate that it would not suit him. But the passion of his life was to dominate, to lead, to dictate, and his vehement advice to a young friend reflected his own attitude: "Make to yourself an image, and, in defiance of the decalogue, worship it. Whether it be excellence in medicine or law, or political eminence, determine not to relax your endeavors until you have attained it." [9]

Only, the higher and finer elements, which might have led to solid glory, were thwarted by the terrible defect of temper that soured ambition into dogmatic arrogance and petty vanity. With the keen insight that he applied to himself as well as to others Randolph gauged his weakness and its effects: "I know neither how to conciliate the love nor to command the esteem of mankind; and like the officious ass in the fable, must bear the blows inflicted on my presumption." [10] The temper in his case was not so much an inflammable anger, which burst out in self-forgetful fury, as a constant, irritable sensitiveness, which stung right and left, like wasps or scorpions, yet was always under the guidance of a fierce clear vision, planting the dart in the most vulnerable spot. It had something of the instinct of vindictive torment which had come to him through Pocahontas from the Indian ancestors in whom he took such pride.

It was indeed largely a matter of nerves, nerves strained and shattered by excess and neglect and passion, the weakness of a body which was never prostrated by illness, yet never well. At one minute he would tell a visitor that he was dying and would take an affectionate farewell of him and of this world. A few hours later the visitor, riding homeward, would be passed by Randolph, in a fury of dust and speed; and with a shout that he was still "dying, dying," he would hurry on to live with more violence than a dozen robuster men.[11] What wonder that such nerves, so treated, made him seem and act like "a man without a skin."[12]

And the nerves, instead of being soothed and quieted, were stimulated by excitement and by alcohol, until their riot at certain times approached definite insanity.[13] Just how much the man drank is difficult to determine. He himself often insists upon periods of almost total abstinence. Others emphasize a disgraceful excess, which, in later years especially, accounted for many of his worst eccentricities both in public and in private. At any rate, it is certain that he drank far too much for the good of a temperament like his. Curiously enough, the book that lay open, as if just read, upon his desk, at the time of his death was a thin duodecimo by one McNish, on Drunkenness.[14]

Worse even for such nerves as Randolph's, worse for his fellows, if not for himself, than the intoxication of alcohol, was the intoxication of words. Such a tongue, stimulated by excitement, urged on by the whirling impetus of a passionate imagination, flew to incredible excesses of abuse. And what aggravated the matter was that clear coolness of brain I have indicated above, which could see that every poisonous word found the palpitating mark it was aimed at. The vision was even so steady that when an opponent lost his temper, it could make use of apology, of conciliation, of apparent humility, with the obvious result of inflicting a deeper wound.[15] And then again the tongue would lash out with that self-provoking fury which the fatal command of language is sure to arouse in nerves that have been strained beyond the power of control.

The bitterness in words with Randolph was much; but it was greatly intensified by the bitterness of manner, a fierce, relentless, domineering, Indian savagery, which tormented its victim all the more when he seemed to cringe and cower. And the manner was rendered far more deadly by the singular appearance of the creature that achieved it. As a child, Randolph is said to have been beautiful.[16] But in manhood all the descriptions make him approach the grotesque. He was tall, he was thin, his body was short, his legs were immensely long, so that when he

rose to speak, he seemed to unfold in endless emaci-
ated longitude. He distorted his features, he con-
torted his limbs. His voice was high-pitched sometimes almost to a shriek; yet he could modulate it so
as to soothe and charm and even to entrance. But
the two points that are most insisted on are the piercing, withering, terrible brightness of his eyes and the
ghostly, blighting use of his long, lean forefinger.
For thirty years the House sat up and listened when
this strange image of an inspired, windmill-smashing
Quixote lectured or scourged it. With such a brain,
and such a tongue, and such a searing eye and cruel
finger, it will readily be seen that Randolph would
have been a strange, conspicuous, and formidable
figure in any governing assembly in the world.

II

HE certainly was so in the House of Representatives,
and in that body substantially his whole career was
one of conflict. It so happened that when he entered
Congress the essentially Southern party, with which
he identified himself, the Republican, was in bitter
opposition to the Federalist rule under John Adams.
Randolph was at once received as a brilliant party
leader, and his singular oratorical powers gave him a
prominent position on that side of the House. At his

age and with his connections, it seemed as if he was assured of a splendid future, perhaps of the highest office in the country. Then the Federalists fell in 1801, and the Republicans, under Jefferson, had a chance to show what their principles amounted to. In Randolph's view they amounted to little. For a time he endeavored honestly to support his chief, and showed what his capacity for useful parliamentary service might have been.[17] Then, to use his own language, "I found I might co-operate, or be an honest man. I have therefore opposed and will oppose them."[18] In other words, compromise, concession, those mutual sacrifices of opinion by which alone constructive work can be done in the world, were distasteful to him. He preferred to stand alone, to accuse as dishonest and disloyal every one who disagreed with him. He could get along with nothing and with nobody, and he had a superb faculty of saying so. The consequence was that he became a political vagrant, sometimes courted, more often dreaded, and in the end too frequently ridiculed, though rarely to his face.

It would be difficult to find any statesman in history who so habitually opposed large measures of public interest. It even seemed as if he preferred opposition to consistency, since he sometimes spoke and voted against himself. He began by attacking the Federalist treaty with England, and his first celebrated utterance is the toast "Damn George Washington!"[19] He attacked the standing army, and got into such hot water as might be expected by calling the regular troops mercenaries and ragamuffins. When Jefferson succeeded to power, Randolph supported him so far as the acquisition of Louisiana; but when the purchase of Florida came, he broke with his party decidedly and in substance forever.

He opposed war with England. He opposed the national bank because he feared it would commercialize the government and everybody connected with it. His attitude towards slavery was in the highest degree curious. He hated it in the abstract, regretted he had ever owned a slave,[20] set all his own slaves free by will,[21] and denounced the slave-trade with his usual virulence.[22] Yet so bitter were his hatred of the Yankee and his antipathy to the professed abolitionist that he became more and more identified with the slave-holding party and perhaps did more to solidify the belligerent South than any one before Calhoun.[23]

Equally contradictory in appearance are his utterances in regard to the national government. He always professed and no doubt felt a profound attachment to the Union. Yet he persistently and furiously fought any attempt to increase the power and influence of the Federal authority. The acquisition of new territory, the admission of new states, above all, large national works of public improvement and the enthusiastic Americanism of Clay were hateful to him, and he never hesitated to say so. In other words, he lived and died an ardent advocate of State Rights, and those of us who still retain a vague affection for that somewhat battered relic of antiquity may find in his speeches many eloquent arguments which are quite as applicable to-day as they were then. At the same time, devoted Virginian though he was, he never hesitated to attack what seemed to him the deplorable backslidings of Virginia.[24] In short, nothing was too dear or too sacred to feel the rough side of his critical tongue. Even religion did not escape. In youth disgust with Christianity made him wish to be a Mohammedan.[25] In later years, though nominally orthodox, he was always ready to dilate upon his abhorrence of prelatical pride and puritanical preciseness.[26]

Perhaps the most striking example of his political prejudices was in regard to the Yazoo land claims. This corrupt transaction of the Georgia legislature is generally admitted to have been as reprehensible as it was complicated. But to Randolph's vivid imagination it became a sort of mythical monster, a political dragon which he was divinely commissioned to slay. Its foul taint had infected every class of society and every branch of government. The very mention of the subject was enough to start him on one of the tirades which filled his friends with terror and even his enemies with admiration. Above all, the mere odd, hideous term, *Yazoo*, was a famous word for him to hiss and shriek and bellow with savage vehemence of blasting look and dooming finger at those whom he detested.

For, ready as he was to attack measures, he was even readier to attack men, and the assault on measures was often but the mask veiling a bitter and long-cherished personal grudge. It is said to have been his boast that he never forgave an enemy and never deserted a friend.[27] The latter statement may be open to question; but forgiveness was not Randolph's strong point. In his odd spurts of religion he made an earnest endeavor for it, and as life went on, he cultivated a milder feeling toward some of those whom he had hated most, "Indeed I wish well to all — I must except a few 'caitiffs' — and would do good to all, if it was in my power"; [28] but the effort was desperate and the caitiffs, in his opinion, were many. When he was a boy, he saw President Adams's coachman snap

a whip over his brother: he never forgave John
Adams.[29] He admired and followed Jefferson at
first. Later he called him "Saint Thomas of Canting-
bury," [30] an epithet apt enough to be intensely dis-
agreeable. With Madison he had little tolerance or
patience at any time, but fought him and abused him
where he could. As long as Monroe could be made an
instrument of this hatred, Randolph was friendly to
Monroe. Later he opposed him like the others: eras
and apostles of good feeling were not the sort of
thing for Randolph. As for John Quincy Adams, certain superficial elements of resemblance between them
only made the fundamental opposition more marked
and the feeling more bitter. "The cub," said Randolph "is a greater bear than the old one." [31]

With all these very lofty personages there could
hardly be any question of personal insult. With men
of less note Randolph's rudeness and brutality often
went to atrocious lengths. He bullied and stormed,
he taunted and scolded, and gained his ends simply
because decent people were reluctant to employ his
methods to retaliate. "Attacks upon the feelings and
opinions of others were one of the means he adopted
of maintaining his supremacy," says a Southern biographer. [32] More or less legendary stories illustrate
the feeling about him in Washington, like that re-

corded by Manasseh Cutler, who tells of Randolph's outburst of resentment at a dinner party. After escorting the ladies from the room, he "took a wineglass filled, and dashed the wine into Alston's eyes and broke the glass to pieces over his head; after some bustle, he took up a gin-bottle and dashed it at him and left the room." [33]

It would naturally be supposed that such performances would have meant an endless succession of duels. Why they did not is a puzzle. Randolph's physical courage is wholly beyond dispute. But naturally he had no desire to be shot, and he seems to have let his cool brain manage his quarrels with nicety and stop his irritable nerves just at the limit of provocation. His own opinion of the duel in the abstract was inclined to be condemnatory; [34] but his attitude reminds one of the charming remark of Barbey d'Aurevilly, when an adversary taunted him with being restrained by religion: "Sir, I have always put my passions above my principles: I am at your orders." In any case, Randolph was perpetually upon the verge of fighting. Combat seemed to be more or less imminent with Wilkinson, with Jefferson's son-in-law, T. M. Randolph, with Eppes. But in all these instances disaster appears to have been averted by the beneficent virtue of an if. The most

curious case is the altercation with Daniel Webster.
For some cause, or more likely for none, Randolph,
early in 1816, sent a challenge. Webster simply
crushed him, writing: "It is enough that I do not
feel myself bound at all times and under any circumstances, to accept from any man, who shall choose to
risk his own life, an invitation of this sort; although
I shall always be prepared to repel in a suitable manner the aggression of any man who may presume upon
such a refusal." [35] The odd thing is that, after the
affair was patched up, Webster had the Olympian
impertinence to write to Randolph requesting a copy
of his own note, and odder still is the almost whee-
dling courtesy with which Randolph sends it, and replies: "I now regret very much that I did not leave
Georgetown with you this morning. I have just
dined where you breakfasted this morning with a
most pleasant party." [36] This strange creature could
caress and even flatter, when the mood took him.

On only two occasions, so far as the records go,
did Randolph actually appear in the dueling field,
and on both his courage was unimpeachable. The
first was an affair at college. The second was the
historical duel in 1826 with Henry Clay, whom Randolph had bracketed with President John Quincy
Adams as a combination of blackleg and Puritan.[37]

Randolph's conduct was characteristic. He solemnly assured his second beforehand that on no account would he fire at Clay. Then, on the ground, he intimated that he might change his mind. Then his pistol went off too soon. Then, having received Clay's fire through the white flannel wrapper, which he persisted in wearing [38] — as Sainte-Beuve fought his only duel under an umbrella — he shook hands with his adversary with the utmost cordiality. And the delicious epilogue to the whole thing is furnished by Benton, who gives a detailed account of it: "It was about the last high-toned duel that I have witnessed, and among the highest-toned that I have ever witnessed." [39]

Nor was it enough for Randolph to be at odds with the whole political world about him. He was perpetually at odds with his own soul. In one of the many brilliant pages of his brilliant biography Henry Adams points out what a multiplicity of conflicts the man carried all the time within.[40] He was a slaveholder and a lover of liberty. He was an aristocrat and a lover of democracy. He was an individualist and he worshiped the establishment of authority and power. Most fundamental of all, he was an intense conservative. It was "a great cardinal principle," he declared, "that should govern all statesmen — never, without the strongest necessity, to disturb that which was at rest." [41] And surely this is the essence of conservatism, to hate change, to love quiet, to seek repose. But repose was about as compatible with the soul of John Randolph as with the soul of Satan.

So the incorrigible quarreler kept up a constant, exhausting, devouring quarrel, even with himself. And if it be true that conflict, both external and internal, is the secret of tragedy, Randolph is one of the most truly tragic figures that the world has seen.

III

WE have followed this perturbed spirit in the eccentric gyrations of its public activity. Its movements in the private and personal sphere, where it should have found distraction and relief, are not less interesting to investigate. Let us take first the external relations and contacts with other human beings, then the varied and complex and subtle inner life.

Randolph was a Virginian planter. He acquired by inheritance and purchase vast amounts of real estate. He had a great number of slaves and live-stock of all kinds. He raised tobacco and various other crops and his letters are full of allusion to agricultural doings. His business management seems to have been sufficiently practical and his bachelor housekeeping simple but tidy. Yet he did not like the life. "My plantation affairs, always irksome, are now revolting," he writes in 1814.[42] At any rate, they gave him a good deal to think of. When he was a boy, his mother said to him: "Keep your land, and your land will keep you." [43] The passion for keeping it grew to be almost a mania. Unfortunately land does not mean money. As Randolph's acres increased, his cash diminished. This embarrassed him, exasperated him, and in his later years drove him to what seemed like positive avarice, though no one could declaim more bitterly against the greed for money than he did.[44]

As to his slaves, his attitude is much what one would expect. He had a profound pity and even tenderness for them in the abstract, did what he could for their comfort, and in some respects felt in their real affection a human intimacy that he discovered nowhere else: "in these poor slaves I have found my best and most faithful friends."[45] Yet he did not hesitate to bully them, to punish them severely, and with his irritable, jealous, and suspicious temper it was unavoidable that he should be constantly scolding them when he knew that he should be scolding himself, and accusing them of crimes that had occurred only in his own imagination. Listen to the strange yet characteristic harangue that he delivered to them after his return from Russia: "After all my superior kindness, when I was in my feeble health, sent a minister to Russia, you all thought I would not live to return, and you and the overseers (damn you — God forgive me) wasted and stole all you could and came well nigh ruining me. But come back, and I will forgive; come back to God, and he will forgive." [46]

As was natural in such surroundings, the man's life was largely occupied with field sports. He liked to roam with his gun, to tire out thought, if he could not get rid of it. In his own pretty phrase, "Bodily motion seems to be some relief to mental uneasiness, and I was delighted yesterday morning to hear that the snipes are come." [47] Though he killed the wild creatures, he had a strange tenderness for them and with tears in his eyes told a friend of finding two little hares that had been hanged by the neck. [48] He loved his dogs and his horses and had quantities of them, liked to ride and drive the wildest of them at breakneck risk, and talked of them with affection on his deathbed.

He was quick and keen at indoor sports also, played an excellent hand of whist, and was expert at chess. He himself ironically declared that the hatred which he imagined that Jefferson entertained for him originated in a lost game of chess.⁴⁹ Perhaps there were other more substantial causes. But indoor games meant contact and conflict with other human beings, and in all these social relations Randolph's peculiarities at once asserted themselves. His terrible, bitter tongue would not be controlled and its savage outbursts were as embarrassing for the spectators as they were painful for the victims. Take one little scene, recounted by Ticknor, the tilt with the Abbé Correa, who had expressed some surprise that he had not found more Virginian gentlemen residing in luxury on their plantations. "Perhaps, Mr. Correa," said Randolph, "your acquaintance was not so much with that class of persons." Correa, who was naturally courteous, answered: "Perhaps not; the next time I will go down upon the Roanoke, and I will visit Mr. Randolph and his friends." Then came the Randolph retort: "In *my* part of the country, gentlemen commonly wait to be *invited* before they make visits." Correa delayed a moment, till every one was listening, then observed quietly: "Said I not well of the *gentlemen* of Virginia?" ⁵⁰

And these eccentricities of temper were accentuated by oddities of dress and manner, as well as by the inborn oddity of appearance, which tended to make the man ridiculed when he was not disliked.

His behavior at the Russian Imperial Court gave rise to many, perhaps mythical,[51] legends not creditable to his country or himself. Curiously enough in England he was popular. For one thing, his aristocratic instinct delighted in the society of peers and peeresses. And then, as Irving points out, he was one of the first Americans to profit by the fact that "in high life here they are always eager after everything strange and peculiar." [52] As Trinculo justly remarks, "Were I in England now . . . there would this monster make a man. Any strange beast there makes a man."

Still, it must be confessed that if Randolph's social surface was odd and repellent, he had some qualities that always succeed. He had wide knowledge of the world and a keen insight to profit by that knowledge. He had a rich and varied vocabulary and a ready and vivid wit. He seems to have been most successful when he had the talk to himself, and Irving tells us that at a dinner with Sydney Smith and other London wits Randolph did not shine. [53] He confessed this weakness, with the candor which is one of his chief charms, when he said to Josiah Quincy, "As the son of a valued friend of mine, it has given me great pleasure to talk with you. I mean to talk *to* you, for I have given you no chance to say five words this evening." [54] But when you let him have his way and listened respectfully, you were bound to be so delighted and instructed that the hours slipped by unnoticed.

And one other attractive trait is recorded of him in social intimacy: "*When alone* with a friend he would not only bear with patience, but would invite a full expression of his friend's opinion on his conduct, or acts and sentiments, on any subject, either private or public." [55] Unfortunately the list of friends with whom this trait might be manifested was shifting and variable. I have already quoted Randolph's remark that he never lost a friend. But somehow, although at different times he had numerous close associates, they all drifted away from him. Dr. Brockenborough seems to have held his attachment to the last. But men in general, however well disposed, found continued intimacy with him difficult. Yet he himself declared, perhaps with truth, that he had a passionate desire for affection. "The necessity of 'loving and being beloved,' was never felt by the imaginary beings of Rousseau and Byron's creation more imperiously than by myself." [56] Only, he was too prone to blame others for not responding to such affection, when it was his own peculiar mental twist that made the response impossible. "The world has used me so ill," he writes to a young relative

" — yet why blame the world? Those from whom I had a right to expect a very different conduct, have betrayed such shameless selfishness, so bare-faced a disregard of my feelings, and of *my rights*, that, but for you, I should sink into inveterate misanthropy." [57] *My rights* is italicised by the man himself: pity that so often undue emphasis upon our rights should account amply for a world of imagined wrongs.

And woman delighted him not neither, though by your smiling you seem to say so. His rule appears to have been the excellent one of the "Imitation": "be not a friend to any one woman, but recommend all good women in general to God." He spoke well of the sex at large and praised their social influence, [58] at the same time deprecating anything that interfered with their duties in the nursery and by the fireside. [59] But his general abstinence from intimate relations with women agrees with a well-attested physical disability, [60] which might be connected with many of his eccentricities. One obscure yet passionate love affair seems indeed to have cast a haunting shadow over his whole life. The attachment was returned and its intensity is well indicated in Randolph's own words: "My apathy is not natural, but superinduced. There *was* a volcano under my ice, but it is burnt out, and a face of desolation has come on, not to be rectified in ages, could my life be prolonged to a patriarchal longevity." [61] Again, he speaks with startling energy of "*one* I loved better than my own soul, or him that created it." [62] A marriage was arranged, but the details are mysterious, not to say mythical, and no authentic explanation of the final rupture is available. [63]

It might at least have been hoped that one so humanly isolated would have had members of his family about him to alleviate the hostility or indifference of the world. But it was not so. Randolph himself gives a highly colored picture of the situation: "My dear child, when I look back upon the past, the eventful history of my race and name (now fast verging towards extinction) presents a tragedy that far outstrips in improbability and rivals in horror all dramatic or romantic fiction." [64] But the facts were highly colored enough. His father died young. His mother married again and then died young enough for her son to worship her memory. But he quarreled bitterly with his stepfather over money and this more or less estranged him from his half-brothers. His own brother, whom he adored, died early. Randolph promptly quarreled with the brother's widow and had a bitter feud with her sister, who was involved in an atrocious family scandal. [65] Of the two nephews, who were his only hope for perpetuating his infinite pride of race, one was deaf and dumb and finally imbecile, and the other died of consumption at an early age. The letters addressed to his niece Elizabeth are full of a charming tenderness,[66] but no young girl could have entered very deeply into Randolph's later life. A relative named Dudley was for many years an object of generosity, devotion, and solicitude, and again of insane caprice.[67] But later he also sinks from view, and Randolph's deathbed was surrounded by none but slaves and strangers. His spirit of melancholy prophecy seems hardly to have exaggerated when at the time of the Clay duel he declared, on refusing to fire at his adversary because of his wife and children: "Their tears would be shed over his grave; but when the sod of Virginia rests on my bosom, there is not in this wide world one individual to pay this tribute upon mine."[68]

IV

So the tortured soul got little comfort out of humanity. Did it get more out of itself? Unquestionably it was rich in spiritual resources, in those possibilities of diversion or distraction which are the most reliable and satisfactory because they are the most within our power, — provided only we have the wisdom and the self-command to make use of them. Randolph was keenly alive to artistic beauty. When he was in England, he delighted in painting and tells us, with his characteristic vanity, that "I astonished some of their connoisseurs as much by the facility with which I pointed out the hand of a particular master, without reference to the catalogue . . . as by my exact knowledge of the geography, topography, and statistics of the country." [69] Especially he enjoyed music, and might have made it a mighty instrument of spiritual relaxation. But here again the old wilful, aristocratic perversity stepped in, and he would not condescend to cultivate his gifts: "This is owing in a great measure to the low estimate that I saw the fiddling, piping gentry held in when I was young." [70]

In the same way, he was an immense reader, from his childhood made himself roughly conversant with the great writers of the world. He was critical, discriminating, nicely insistent upon fine points of correctness, and when he was mortally ill he reprimanded a friend who was reading to him for a mispronunciation.[71] Yet his reading and his thinking were disorderly, irrelevant, incoherent. He would have scorned to set himself with system to any scholarly task, and in consequence he was accustomed to refer to himself, of course with gross injustice, as "an ignorant man." [72] The poets he always loved and

148

often quoted; but is it not characteristic that his favorite Shakespearean plays were *Lear* and *Timon?* [73]

The study of Randolph's religion is as curious as that of his intelligence. In his youth he inclined to infidelity; but this was more a matter of emotional rebellion than of profound thought, and he soon returned, at least nominally, to the religion that his mother taught him. For a period of years he even took the matter with intense seriousness, and for a much briefer period he thought himself converted and saw some spiritual light. Just how far this affected his conduct is another question, though he is said to have sensibly reduced the profanity of his language. But even at this time his religion appears to have brought him neither comfort nor serenity; and for the most part it added only another agitation to that turbulent temper which could never be still. Sometimes he doubted as to the essential truth. Sometimes, even granting salvation by the truth, he doubted whether it could ever be for him. "I fear that I mistake a sense of my sins for true repentance, and that I sometimes presume upon the mercy of God. Again, it appears incredible that one so contrite as I sometimes know myself to be, should be rejected entirely by infinite mercy." [74] In his agony he seemed to feel something of the strange distress

which afflicted the poet Cowper, when he was persuaded that the blessing of the Almighty had abandoned him forever: "There are times . . . when the
chaos of my mind can be compared with nothing but
the state that poor Cowper was in before he found
peace." [75]

So, in spite of beauty and books and even God,
Randolph's prevailing spiritual tone was one of grief
and wretchedness. Our friends the psychoanalysts
may apply their theories to account for this: there
can be no dispute as to the fact. The man has start-
lingly vivid and telling ways of expressing his mental
state. "I often mount my horse and sit upon him ten
or fifteen minutes, wishing to go somewhere but not
knowing where to ride, for I would escape anywhere
from the incubus that weighs me down, body and
soul; but the fiend follows me 'ex croupa.' You can
have no conception of the intenseness of this wretchedness, which in its effect on my mind I can compare to nothing but that of a lump of ice on the pulse
of the wrist, which I have tried when a boy." [76] And
again, "My good friend, I can't convey to you —
language can't express — the thousandth part of the
misery I feel." [77]

It is clear that such a condition of nerves and
spirits must have been intimately connected with the

wear and tear of indigestion and other physical weakness. Randolph repeatedly goes into a technical discussion of his ailments, which is curious, and sometimes wearisome. The intense excitement of some of his pursuits necessarily reacted into a correspondingly intense depression, and the resort to alcohol, and in later years to morphine, obviously did not help.

The wretchedness and despair were further aggravated by the solitude in which he lived. From his few months of busy interest in Washington he would pass to the utter isolation of his Roanoke home. Nature was about him and in a manner he loved it. But there was too much of it. The deep forests, the vast meadows, the sluggish streams overclouded his soul and made its shadows deeper. He knew the defect, he saw the danger; yet, as such minds do, he sought it all the more. "The darkness of my hours, so far from having passed away, has thickened into the deepest gloom. I try not to think, by moulding my mind upon the thoughts of others; but to little purpose. Have you ever read Zimmerman on Solitude? I do not mean the popular cheap book under that title, but another, in which solitude is considered with respect to its dangerous *influence* upon the mind and the heart." [78] And he knew well

151

that the material solitude was nothing to the profounder spiritual solitude which he himself had created: "I feel that in this world I am alone — that all my efforts (ill-judged and misdirected I am willing to allow they must have been) have proved abortive. What remains of my life must be spent in a cold and heartless intercourse with mankind, compared with which the solitude of Robinson Crusoe was bliss. I have no longer a friend." [79]

He had lost his faith in his fellow men. He had asked too much of life, and because it could not give him all he asked, he condemned it entirely. As with so many noble natures, his ideal of friendship and of human conduct generally was too high. When men came short of it, he could see no good in them at all. The bitterness of his misanthropy approaches that of Timon: "For three days past, I have rode out, and people who would not care one groat, if I died to-night — are glad that I am so much better, &c., &c., with all that wretched grimace that grown-up makers of faces call, and believe to be, politeness, good-breeding, &c. I had rather see the children or monkeys mow and chatter." [80]

He had lost his faith in the world, in its present, in its future. His innate conservatism made him imagine some good in the past. But the times he was

obliged to live in were bad, and he could see no hope
of their improving. "Let us not disguise the fact, sir,
we think we are living in the better times of the Republic. We deceive ourselves; we are almost in the
days of Sylla and Marius: yes, we have almost got
down to the time of Jugurtha." [81] For a confirmed
idealist, whose dreams were of perfection, who would
not be satisfied with less than heaven, if even with
that, the mingled world we live in was horror and
anathema: "I am more and more convinced that,
with a few exceptions, this world of ours is a vast
madhouse. The only men I ever knew well, ever
approached closely, whom I did not discover to be
unhappy, are sincere believers of the Gospel, and con-
form their lives, as far as the nature of man will per-
mit, to its precepts. There are only *three* of them." [82]

It will be seen that in many aspects of this brooding
despair Randolph suggests the great European romantics, Rousseau, Byron, Obermann, Leopardi; and
in his power of expressing his spiritual state he is not
altogether unworthy to be compared with them. He
has their egotistical tendency to regard himself as
distinct, peculiar, set apart from the common herd.
He has their disposition to hint at mystery in his own
life, some strange, secret, unutterable cause of grief,
which cannot be escaped or shaken off. It might be

remorse, it might be love, it might be the incapacity of loving. We are only to understand that it is something obscure and terrible. Again, Randolph is like the romantics in his lack of humor. He takes himself with constant seriousness and would have us take him so, does not get those glimpses of his own comic insignificance in the face of eternity which save a temper like Lamb's from utter despair.

What differentiates Randolph from the European group is his partial, and for the time intense, preoccupation with active life. He emerged from his solitude and played a fiercely busy part in the affairs of men, as if the world were worth saving, as if human hearts were worth loving, as if his keen and powerful intelligence were created to be really useful and not self-destructive. Then he withdrew again, and the cloud descended upon him, blacker and more blighting than ever. It was not only that life was hideous, immoral, and altogether unworthy: it was far worse, it was empty. "I can no longer imagine any state of things under which I should not be wretched. I mean a possible state. I am unable to enter into the conceptions and views of those around me. They talk to me of grave matters, and I see children blowing bubbles." [83]

In short, we have one more example of a rich and

powerful and much endowed spirit endlessly and use-
lessly tormenting itself. The man had every external
means to happiness: wealth, social position, early
glory, almost unlimited prestige. They were all
soured, embittered, and turned to poison by lack of
control over the inner world. And the interest of the
case is greatly heightened by his own perfect com-
prehension and clear exposition of it. Again and
again he enjoins upon others to avoid the abyss into
which he has fallen. "Struggle against desponding
and low spirits, and endeavor to cultivate and to
cherish a cheerful, or, at least, a serene, habit of mind.
This is more in our power than we are in general aware
of: especially in early life." [84] Alas, the knowledge
had come too late for him to make use of it; the clear
vision might profit others, it could not profit himself.
"We have all two educations; one we have given to
us — the other we give ourselves; and after a certain
time of life, when the character has taken its *ply*, it
is idle to attempt to change it." [85]

The concluding lines of Landor's admirable dia-
logue between Rousseau and Malesherbes apply forcibly to Randolph, and, alas, to how many others.
Malesherbes says, "It is as much at your arbitra-
tion on what theme you shall meditate, as in what
meadow you shall botanize; and you have as much at

your option the choice of your thoughts, as of the keys in your harpsichord." To which Rousseau objects, "If this were true, who could be unhappy?" And the answer is: "Those of whom it is not true. Those who from want of practice cannot manage their thoughts, who have few to select from, and who, because of their sloth or of their weakness, do not roll away the heaviest from before them."

VI
JOHN BROWN

CHRONOLOGY

Born, Torrington, Litchfield County, Connecticut, May 9, 1800.
Married Dianthe Lusk, June 21, 1820.
Various business ventures and migrations, 1820–1855.
Wife died, August 10, 1832.
Married Mary Anne Day, 1833.
Arrived in Kansas, October, 1855.
Pottawatomie murders, May 24, 1856.
Chatham Convention, April–May, 1858.
Carried slaves to Canada, February–March, 1859.
Established at Kennedy Farm, July, 1859.
Raid began, October 16, 1859.
Captured, October 18, 1859.
Sentenced, November 2, 1859.
Executed, Charlestown, Virginia, December 2, 1859.

VI

JOHN BROWN

I

It is always profoundly interesting to study a controversy where there is right on both sides, though neither can see the right in the other. In the American Civil War the South, with however little fault of its own, was oppressed, smothered by the hideous burden of slavery. On the other hand, it was contending for the original principle of state vitality, the most important element in our Constitution, and one steadily undermined by Federal encroachment and above all by the War.

Up to 1861 the most intense complication of these contending principles was in Kansas. There right and wrong fought their battle with furious bitterness and with a heat of wrath and recrimination which is as pitiful as it is fascinating to behold. And into this thick and bushy tangle of motives and passions John Brown hewed unhesitatingly with the fierce and cruel axe of his unfaltering will. But, as it happens, Brown himself is as complex a puzzle as Kansas, and friends and enemies have torn his memory to pieces in the effort to make him out devil or saint; whereas he was neither, but a human being, with immense aspirations and hopes and struggles, like you or me. In any case, he was perhaps the most curious American example of the intensity of fanatical enthusiasm, and as such the analysis of his soul, with its damage and its glory, has a profound and absorbing interest.

Before beginning such analysis, however, we must have a brief summary of his remarkable career, avoiding controversy as much as is possible, where many facts and almost all motives are subject to contest. In making such a summary, we must first acknowledge indebtedness to the admirable biography of Mr. Villard, whose thoroughness of research is equaled only by his obvious desire to be fair to all parties and all men.

Brown was born in Connecticut in 1800. His parents were of English and Dutch stock and his stubbornness through life did not belie his heredity. He had a severe and sternly nurtured youth, growing up with the Bible in one hand and the plough in the other. In later life he wrote a brief autobiography, which depicts the struggles of his youth in the terse, tense, rude English he always used. All through it you can see the earnest, passionate, obstinate boy, with his soul set on one object, all the more furiously when he found himself balked.

The boy was married when a boy, chased fortune in

strange fashion all over the country, as a tanner, as a surveyor, as a cattle-breeder, as a wool-merchant, and never once caught her. He had and bred and lost children, lost his wife, married another and had more children, illimitably. How he fed them all is a puzzle. But their feeding was simple, and their lives were simple, and their souls were simple, like his, if all souls were not so bewilderingly complex. Through these financial struggles it comes out increasingly evident that Brown was not a good man of business, though often shrewd and practical, as in his skilful classification of wools. His temperament was speculative, fed on high hopes, if little else. He worked with borrowed capital, his schemes failed, and he came to grief, like many others. Most of us believe that he was fundamentally honest. But some do not. It may be well to quote here the most scathing piece of abuse that I have met with, as an antidote to much that will come later: "I knew the old scoundrel long before the war; long before Kansas was known; long before abolition had many advocates. He tried to blow up his mother-in-law with powder; he was guilty of every meanness. He involved his father at one time in ruin, and everybody else he had anything to do with." [1] So do the saints and martyrs appear to those who have suffered by them.

But if the practical world rejected Brown and misunderstood him, the unpractical had its revenge in yielding him immortal glory. He gave his life with mad abandonment to the American negro and that sacrifice raised him on a pedestal no envy and no detraction will ever throw down. Just when Brown's devotion to the abolition cause began cannot be definitely settled. In later years he and his family placed it very early. Mr. H. P. Wilson, who has dissected Brown's soul with searching and ingenious cruelty, but I think with utter misapprehension, believes that this early origin was invented, [2] and that Brown's anti-slavery enthusiasm was merely a hypocritical mask, to conceal the old greed for gain which had been in so many ways disappointed. I do not see how any one who has studied Brown's life and letters with care can question his sincerity for a moment, and I believe, after a consideration of all the evidence, that the passion for freeing the slaves was early conceived and grew and broadened with years until, when he was nearly sixty years old, it broke out in the wild adventures of Kansas and Harper's Ferry.

Several of Brown's sons went to Kansas in 1854 and 1855. They were led in part, no doubt, by the enthusiasm of the free-soil movement, largely also by the instinct of adventure and of seeking fortune under new conditions. Their father was interested in their project from the first. He heard of the violence and aggression of the pro-slavery men, who were thronging into the territory from Missouri, left his wife and other children at his farm in North Elba, New York, and made his way to Kansas, well-armed, eager to help his sons, and passionately curious to see what would turn up. When he arrived, the struggle between the political parties was violently under way. Accounts vary as to the prominence of his earlier part in it. He was never a man to work with others, much less under them. He could contend, command, control: he could not obey. At any rate, he was intimately involved in the furious complications of the end of 1855 and the beginning of 1856, and his antipathy to the advocates of slavery increased in bitterness, if it could. There was wrath and recrimination everywhere, some unwarranted violence, and a luxury of threats, meaning much or little, but all serving to foment hatred. Brown made up his mind that a cruel example was needed. In May, 1856, he and a party of his followers took by night five pro-slavery men from among their Pottawatomie neighbors, men of bad character but not more criminal than others, and butchered them, literally hacked them to pieces with cutlasses. Brown always insisted, in a fashion approaching duplicity, that he had no actual hand in the deed; but the whole responsibility was his. In any case, it was a bloody, brutal murder, and quite without immediate excuse. Brown's admirers declare that it saved Kansas to freedom. Less prejudiced historians believe that it did more harm than good.

Brown's course in the West after Pottawatomie was much what it had been before. He was engaged in several so-called battles, with a few men on each side, and behaved always with absolute intrepidity and sometimes with shrewdness. Mr. Wilson insists that his chief motive was plunder. There was plenty of disreputable plundering on both sides, horse-stealing in particular. But there can be no serious doubt that Brown regarded it all as a worthy despoiling of the Egyptians and intended religiously to devote all profit to the advancement of the cause.

In the autumn of 1856 Brown left Kansas. The year 1857 he spent in the Middle West and East, gathering funds and arousing enthusiasm in various societies and individuals, with the ostensible purpose of aiding in the Kansas struggle, but with at any rate some further and deeper plans for a more central attack upon the strongholds of slavery. In the summer of 1858 he returned to Kansas, where conditions were again acute, made a raid into Missouri, captured a considerable

number of slaves, and, after a journey full of picturesque vicissitudes, carried them triumphantly to
Canada where the British flag ensured their permanent freedom. John Brown never entered Kansas
again.

II

As there is endless controversy over the date of
Brown's first interest in slavery, so historians dispute
over his conception of the Harper's Ferry adventure.
If the conversation recorded by Frederick Douglass
as having taken place in 1847 is to be accepted [3] —
and I think it must be in substance — Brown was at
that time brooding over the details of some such
scheme as he afterwards attempted to carry out. He
explained to Douglass this plan for subsisting an
army of whites and blacks in the mountain fastnesses
and so gradually undermining the whole slave power.
In 1849 he made a brief trip to Europe for business
objects and he appears to have attempted a more or
less extensive study of battles and battle-fields with a
military purpose in mind. For, though he was profoundly religious and by profession a hater of war,
like many another such he was a born fighter, and relished nothing more than to have God put a scourge
into his hands to lash the devil.

His daughter testifies explicitly that he told her of his Harper's Ferry plan before he first went to Kansas.[4] In the interval between his two Kansas visits the general outline of the scheme was certainly made more or less plain to some of his Eastern supporters. And in May, 1858, took place in Chatham, Canada, that singular convention of a few whites and a larger number of negroes, which adopted the still more singular Provisional Constitution,[5] Brown's elaborate device for governing the nation within a nation that was to be established by the gradual freeing of the Southern slaves. This instrument, with its lofty tone and its complicated discrimination of executive, legislature, judiciary, etc., seems like a Utopian parody of the Constitution of the United States, developed by a slow, thorough, narrow, limited intellect possessed and obsessed by one idea, and such was assuredly Brown's.

Any hope the inventor of this system may have had of putting it immediately into practice was thwarted by the defection of the restless, unreliable adventurer Forbes, who, after being more trusted by his leader than was any one else, deserted the cause and made perilous revelations as to the methods. Brown was obliged to defer action for a year; but his patience was as indomitable as his energy. "Young

men must learn to wait. Patience is the hardest lesson to learn. I have waited for twenty years to accomplish my purpose." *

At last in the summer of 1859 Brown settled himself and his little band of followers at the Kennedy
Farm in Maryland, about five miles from Harper's
Ferry. The followers were a somewhat heterogeneous
collection. They were by no means all religious men.
Perhaps they had not all been virtuous men. They
were hardy, vigorous young fellows, ready to risk
anything and go anywhere. Most, if not all, of them,
had a superstitious horror of slavery. And every one
of them adored the old man and was willing to die
for him. Just what plan of campaign Brown had
adopted, if any definite, will never be known. His
friends and his enemies have ingeniously supplied him
with several and supported them with what they
think are conclusive arguments. But the arguments
are as different as the conclusions and none is convincing. Somehow or other Brown hoped to gather
a nucleus of slaves and whites whose determined
action in seizing Harper's Ferry would finally lead
to the liberation of every Southern negro. But the
method of accomplishing this is obscure, and we are
obliged largely to fall back upon Brown's trust in the
guidance of God. On the one hand we are told by

Salmon Brown that "Father had a peculiarity of insisting on *order*. I felt that at Harper's Ferry this very thing would be likely to trap him. He would insist on getting everything arranged just to suit him before he would consent to make a move." [7] On the other hand, we have Brown's own impressive saying: "It is an invariable rule *with me* to be governed by circumstances; or in other words *not to do anything* while *I do not know what to do*." [8] No doubt these two positions may be reconciled, but they do not make our puzzle much clearer.

At any rate, the conspirators, about twenty in all, lurked at the Kennedy Farm till the middle of October, slowly accumulating arms and supplies and keeping themselves marvelously hidden from the neighbors' curiosity. Then, on the evening of Sunday, October 16th, Brown marched out, at the head of a petty band of adventurers, to challenge deliberately a great nation by assaulting its officers and seizing its property. The complicated evolutions of Sunday night and Monday need not be traced in detail. By Monday night not only the town of Harper's Ferry but the State of Virginia and the whole country had been aroused and had grasped, at least vaguely, the enormous effrontery of Brown's undertaking. Various peaceful citizens had been killed as well as several of Brown's followers. He himself, after getting possession of the different government buildings and picking up from the surrounding country a number of slaves and also a number of slaveholders as hostages, among whom was a member of the family of Washington, was forced to take refuge, with the remains of his band and his prisoners, in the engine-house, and continued there till Tuesday morning. But in the dull gray October dawn a detachment of United States Marines, under Colonel Robert E. Lee, broke in the doors, liberated the prisoners, and killed or captured all of the defenders. Brown was cut down fighting and received several wounds, which were at first thought to be dangerous, but which afterwards proved to be comparatively unimportant.

Virginia and the whole South were naturally infuriated. Brown was speedily tried on various charges and sentenced to be hanged. His Northern friends complained of indecent haste in the proceedings, but later historians agree that on the whole the affair was conducted with as much consideration as could have been expected. Brown bore himself through it all with the admirable dignity that he had shown from the first moment of his capture. Indeed the testimony of his captors and interrogators to his composure and clear-headedness is as impressive as that of his prisoners to his courage and thoughtful humanity.

During the long weeks of his imprisonment the condemned traitor showed an unfailing self-possession. He discouraged all attempts at escape and urged upon his friends that as a martyr to the cause he would serve it more substantially than by any further living effort. He corresponded widely, and his numerous letters, with their poignant directness and incontrovertible sincerity, afford the best evidence of the great qualities of his character.

On the second of December, 1859, John Brown was hanged at Charlestown, Virginia. Great military preparations were made to ensure a peaceful execution of the sentence and it was carried out with every detail of decorum and decency, except that a painful delay at the last moment prolonged the prisoner's suspense. Brown's bearing was perfect, his courage and calmness without flaw. There were no heroics, no rhetoric. He took an affectionate leave of his companions in arms and gave them each a quarter of a dollar, saying that he should have no further use for money.[9] Of an equally touching simplicity were his words, as he was driven to the gallows: "This *is* a beautiful country. I never had the pleasure of seeing it before,"[10] and the phrase seems somehow to give a startling insight into the vivid and intense perception of a man who is opening his eyes upon the other world. A few hours later the eyes were closed to this, and John Brown had become a strange, great legendary figure in the complicated progress of humanity.

III

So died a typical incarnation of ideal, or fanatical, enthusiasm, a man absolutely convinced of the truth and justice of his own ideas of right and wrong, in certain points at any rate, and determined to impose them upon the world, by persuasion if possible, if not, by bloodshed, agony, and slaughter. He was a theorist, a reasoner, all the more rigorous in his theories because their scope was limited and their range narrow. You can see the rigor in the face, especially before it was bearded, in the set mouth, the cavernous eyes, the sturdy chin, the drawn brows and square forehead. There was a tremendous, indomitable stubbornness in the man. "Let the grand reason, that one course is right and another wrong, be kept continually before your own mind."[11] He kept it always before his and walked straight on, no matter whom his footsteps shattered.

To minds of a different type, reflective, curious, analytical, there is endless interest in studying such a temperament, in weighing the good and evil of its working in the world, good and evil to itself, good and evil to the vast body of its fellow beings. Let us trace out some of the ramifications of this, as illustrated in the case of Brown.

First as to the evil, and the evil to the world at large. Such natures are intolerant, from their point of view they have the right to be so. They know what should be done and what should not. Paltry excuses, quibbling reserves, charitable allowances, what are they but devices of the Evil One, cunningly assorted to obscure the real issue between heaven and hell? "I believe in the Golden Rule and the Declaration of Independence," said Brown. "I think they both mean the same thing; and it is better that a whole generation should pass off the face of the earth — men, women, and children — by a violent death, than that one jot of either should fail *in this country*. I mean exactly *so*, sir." [12] He meant so, he acted so, he lived so.

Such intolerance kills the quiet ease and joy of life. It kills compromise and mutual understanding, and breeds suspicion and mistrust. It breeds wrath and violence, sets father against son and brother against brother, triumphantly justifies such hideous crimes as the brutal murders on the Pottawatomie.

And, alas, so often, it does all this from misapprehension, from reasoning with fierce, narrow, unenlightened logic, and reasoning wrong.

The injury of this fanatical temperament to the individual possessor of it is even more obvious than the injury to the world at large. Take intelligence. It cuts him off from curious knowledge, from wide interest in the movement of life and its varied currents and subtle developments. It makes him feel that all that does not renovate society from his point of view is frivolous and contemptible. Brown read, oh, yes, he read the Bible, always the Bible, and he read Plutarch, and he read books on military science. What if he had read Plato or Montaigne?

And beauty? What room, what leisure is there for beauty, a frivolous distraction, an idle, subtle siren which leads the soul astray from the one clear, arduous path it must forever follow? Brown loved music, loved hymns, they fed his strange melancholy, his strange exaltation. Yet probably he would have said of music, with Cowper: "If it is not used with an unfeigned reference to the worship of God, . . . it degenerates into a sensual delight and becomes a most powerful advocate for the admission of other pleasures, grosser perhaps in degree, but in their kind the same." [13] And Brown loved nature, but we have seen that he walked through it as a man in a dream, and opened his eyes to it only when they were about to close forever.

It was the same with all the comfort of life, ease, fine clothes, delicate food, luxury, grace, elegance, and charm. The grosser man in us, the simple, natural man, unhaunted by far thoughts and tormenting scruples, enjoys these things, savors them, revels in them. But how can any one enjoy them whose mind is forever clouded with the misery of the world? How can a life be happy passed in the midst of those who suffer? To be sure, many lives are; but not this man's. He would cut off human wants, cut off superfluous desires, cut off bare needs. Those poor negroes were toiling under the lash, and why should he achieve felicity? He wore old, plain clothes and ate the simplest sustenance compatible with life. The painter Hunt saw him once at a social gathering refuse oysters "because 'he was not hungry.' I said to a friend — and Brown was not celebrated then, not having been hanged!—'There's something remarkable about that man. Did you ever know a man to refuse oysters at a party because he was not hungry?' He did not take champagne, because he was 'not thirsty.' Held the glass as you would hold a doll for a baby. Was not going to gorge himself — a man with such a destiny and such a work before him." [14] When Douglass visited him in 1847, he was struck with the utter poverty of everything. "Plain as was the outside of this man's house, the inside was plainer .... There was an air of plainness about it which almost suggested destitution." [15] The meal was "such as a man might relish after following the plough all day." [16] "Innocent of paint, veneering, varnish, or table-cloth, the table announced itself unmistakably of pine and of the plainest workmanship." [17] And while the poverty may have resulted in part from lack of business ability, it came far more from absorption in higher things. "For twenty years," said Brown, in 1858, "I have never made any business arrangement which would prevent me at any time answering the call of the Lord. I have kept my affairs in such condition that in two weeks I could wind them up and be ready to obey that call; permitting nothing to stand in the way of duty — neither wife, children, nor worldly goods." [18]

It is equally evident that these lofty spiritual pursuits do not fit well with the lighter side of social life, with the more kindly human relations, the gay exchange of cordial, empty, daily jest and laughter. Brown had a grim, Old Testamentary humor of his own, that relaxed the iron muscles of those mouth-corners just a trifle. But did he ever laugh with abandon? He mingled with men for his own purposes, though even with those closest to him he had a strange and desperate secrecy. For ordinary social converse he had no taste and no aptitude. "I have one unconquerable weakness," he said, with a smile, in those last unsmiling days: "I have always been more afraid of being taken into an evening party of ladies and gentlemen, than of meeting a company of men with guns." [19] Even the faculty of consolation, that most exquisite, tender link of friendship, was denied to him, or at least not given in large measure: "I never seemed to possess a faculty to console and comfort my friends in their grief; I am inclined, like the poor comforters of Job, to sit down in silence, lest in my miserable way I should only add to their grief." [20]

But the crowning interest of the effect of Brown's great aim in life upon his human relations appears in his dealings with his family. He was devotedly attached to both his wives and to his numerous sons and daughters. He was thoughtful of their worldly welfare, as he saw it, to the very end. He was more than thoughtful, he was tender. He was tender to the animals with whom he dealt so much. He was tender, divinely tender with human beings. When those he loved were ill he would give up food, give up

sleep, give up immediately necessary labor to tend
them and watch over them with delicate, considerate
care. Yet he punished with pitiless severity. When
one of his sons had earned a heavy whipping, he inflicted half of it and then made the boy lash the
father's own bare back till the blood came.[21] "He
compelled his wife to ride to church with him on a
pillion on a young and unbroken horse he wished to
tame, with the result that she was twice thrown." [22]

Also, he must rule, dominate, control everything
that came near him. He dominated animals. "He
said that he could always, without moving, make a
dog or cat leave the room if he wished, by his eye." [23]
Was he not one day to be ruler over thousands? If so,
then surely he must dominate at home. "He was intolerant in little things and in little ways. . . . I had
it from [his son] Owen, in a quiet way and from other
sources in quite a loud way that in his family his
methods were of the most arbitrary kind," says a not
too friendly witness.[24] Douglass, a most friendly one,
observes that "he fulfilled Saint Paul's idea of the
head of the family. His wife believed in him, and his
children observed him with reverence." [25]

And when a great cause demanded it, both wife and
children must be sacrificed without a moment's hesitation. He said it often, and, when necessary, he did

it. The little sacrifices were demanded constantly and given freely. The supreme sacrifice was always held in readiness and accorded at the supreme moment. A son was killed in Kansas, two sons were killed at Harper's Ferry. Still he fought on, if not unmoved or without a tear, absolutely unaltered in his resolution to give what was far dearer than his own life to achieving the one great end of his and their existence on this earth. The strain of living so much apart from all he loved was terrible. It wrung his heart to think of their privation and sickness and sorrow. But even this grief was smothered in the thought of all that greater grief: "The anxiety I feel to see my *wife* and children once more I am unable to describe. . . . The *cries* of my poor *sorrow-stricken despairing children*, whose '*tears on their cheeks*' are *ever* in my *eye* and whose *sighs* are *ever* in my ears, may, however, prevent my enjoying the happiness I so much desire." [26]

Truly, the strain of this man's life in the grip of his overpowering obsession illuminates Heine's passionate saying: "We do not have ideas. The Idea has us and enslaves us and scourges us and drives us into the arena to fight for it like gladiators, who combat, whether they will or no." [27]

IV

AND what good comes from this tyrannous mastery of an idea, to balance and compensate all the wide burden of privation and misery? Let us consider such good first as it affects the individual, then as it affects the world at large. To clarify the consideration we must dig a little more deeply into the profound tangle of motives that lies at the base of moral and spiritual, as of all other, effort.

In such a case as Brown's, the persistent, all-excluding nature of the obsession, its constant intrusion in season and out of season, its cruel dominance over all other motives and all other passions, undeniably suggests insanity. This solution has often been urged for Brown. It receives support from the man's singular and unfortunate inheritance. Insanity was rampant in his mother's family and there were a dozen instances in relatives more or less close to him. An effort was made to plead this in court. Brown himself rejected it scornfully. At the same time I think his frequent recurrence to it indicates that its shadow haunted him with some discomfort. "I may be very insane," he wrote; "and I am so, if insane at all. But if that be so, insanity is like a very pleasant dream to me." [28] And again, "If I am insane, of

179

course I should think I know more than all the rest of the world. But I do not think so." " Yet this is precisely what he did think, what every enthusiast and fanatic of his type thinks. In that overmastering, overwhelming assurance of knowing more than all the rest of the world, from whatever source, lies all their power — and all their weakness. In the greatest examples of the type the assurance proves itself well founded. The whole wide world comes in time to think as they did and so to justify their sacrifice and martyrdom. And it is here that more doubt arises in regard to Brown. Strong and vigorous as his intelligence was, it ran so much to the fantastic and the conception, or misconception, of his final effort was so incoherently disastrous, that it is impossible to credit him with clear, commanding intellectual power. At the same time, it is equally impossible to describe him as in the stricter sense insane. Men who reason as consistently and will as insistently and act as persistently as he did, cannot be set apart as of diseased mind.

Yet to subordinate one's whole existence so completely to an all-engrossing purpose is beyond doubt abnormal. It absorbs life, drinks up the soul, sweeps the man out of the common course of daily interests and cares. And precisely in this absorption, in this excitement, lifting you above all earth, lies one of its charms. Such a nature as Brown's is born to struggle and fight, with something, with anything. He thought he loved peace. So he did, in theory. But the peace he loved was the peace you have to fight for. He was eager, restless. To be quiet was death, and to be comfortable, and even to be happy, was too like being quiet. "*I expect nothing* but to 'endure *hardness*,'" he said.[30] He wanted nothing but to endure hardness. When he was enduring and resisting, he knew he was alive. One of the most instructive sentences he ever wrote was, "I felt for a number of years, *in earlier life*, a steady, strong desire *to die;* but since I saw any prospect of becoming a 'reaper' in the *great* harvest, I have not only felt quite willing to *live*, but have enjoyed life much." [31] He probably enjoyed it most of all in prison, when only a few days of it were left him.

And besides the exhilaration of living for an ideal, there is the element of personal ambition. It is quite unnecessary to assume with Mr. Wilson that Brown was actuated entirely by vulgar greed and narrow personal vanity. Who shall say that the greatest of teachers and prophets is wholly exempt from the delight of feeling, if not saying, I did this thing? The man is worth little who has not the root of such ambition in him. Assuredly Brown had it. Did he not write of himself in youth, "He very early in life became ambitious to excel in doing anything he undertook to perform"? [32] Did he not write in age, when treading on the heels of performance, "I have only had *this one* opportunity, in a life of nearly sixty years; and could I be continued ten times as long again, I might not again have another equal opportunity. God has honored but comparatively *a very small* part of mankind with any possible chance for such mighty and soul-satisfying rewards"? [33]

Further, there is the delight of dominance, of controlling things and leading men, of feeling that your sole, petty, finite will is making at least a portion of the universe bow and bend before it. To some spirits the thought of this is hateful and the effort for it repulsive. To others it is the supreme joy of life. And such preëminently was Brown. He even carried the instinct so far as to find it difficult to obey when obedience is perhaps the deepest secret of final mastery. He could not work well with others. He must rule or be nothing. Both friends and enemies testify to this. "Very superstitious, very selfish and very intolerant, with great self esteem. . . . He could not brook a rival," says one witness cited by Mr. Wilson. [34] "He doted on being the head of the heap, and he was," says Brown's brother-in-law.[35] And his son's comment is equally decided: "The trouble is, you want your boys to be brave as tigers, and still afraid of you." [36] While the father, meditating soberly in his Virginia prison, recognized the same weakness as clearly as any one. He writes of one of his sons, he "always has underrated himself; is bashful and retiring in his habits; is not (like his father) too much inclined to assume and dictate." [37]

Thus, such a temper would like to control and dominate the world, but always for the world's good. In Brown at least there was not a trace of conscious desire to rule for evil or for the gratification of any personal motive of mischief or cruelty. In spite of all he had endured and all the slights and injuries of men, he repeats over and over that no thought of revenge enters into any of his efforts. If the wicked must suffer through his action, it is because they are wicked, not because they have tormented him.

For back of all the personal elements, back even of the abstract desire to do good, there was always God, and in the study of such temperaments as Brown's the obscure, vast mystery of God must always be given the largest place. It is here, I think, chiefly that Mr. Wilson's shrewd analysis is at fault. In all the puzzles, in all the tangles, in all the inconsistencies of this strange man's life, especially in elucidating his plan, or lack of plan, before the attack on Harper's Ferry, we must look to God as the solution. He was a child of destiny, like Napoleon, but with him the destiny was the obvious, constant direction of God. "The Lord had directed him in visions what to do." [38] "He scouted the idea of rest while he held 'a commission direct from God Almighty to act against slavery.'" [39] "God had created him to be the deliverer to slaves the same as Moses had delivered the children of Israel." [40] It is true that Brown several times spoke of himself as naturally sceptical.[41] He was shrewd, hard-headed, far from disposed to accept all the fantastic quips and quirks of credulous superstition. But his intense insistence on what he did believe was all the firmer, and he did believe that God had predestined him from eternity to root out the curse from these United States, he did believe that God bade him do fierce and bloody things that that curse might be rooted out forever. In 1856 Mrs. Coleman asked him, "Then, Captain, you think that God uses you as an instrument in his hands to kill men?" And he answered, "I think he has used me as an instrument to kill men; and if I live, I think he will use me as an instrument to kill a good many more." [42]

And if this sense of immediate direction from God,

of being in the hands of God as a mighty agent for his purposes, for everlasting good, even sometimes through apparent evil, is the greatest motive for human accomplishment, is it not also the greatest source of human rapture? The joy it brings is the most acute and exalted of all joys and the peace it gives is the deepest and the most enduring of all peace. So at least Brown found it, in his prison days, with death awaiting him, having failed in his great undertaking according to the judgment of men, but with the growing consciousness that apparent failure covered God's intention in a mightier triumph which could be made perfect only by his departure from this troubled world. He was "fully persuaded that I am worth inconceivably more to *hang* than for any other purpose." [43] And in that persuasion his spirit found more contentment than it had known in all his restless sixty years. "Tell your father that I am quite cheerful; that I do not feel myself in the least degraded by my imprisonment, my chains, or the near prospect of the gallows. Men cannot imprison, or chain, or hang the soul." [44] And when an effort was made to comfort him, he said, "I sleep peacefully as an infant, or if I am wakeful, glorious thoughts come to me, entertaining my mind." [45]

It is one of the characteristics of this spiritual rapture that it is impelled to extend itself to others. None who feels the ecstasy of God upon him can refrain from communicating it, from striving passionately to make the world over and urging others to make it over also. And none strove thus with more ardor than John Brown. Something magnetic in his obsession touched men of the most diverse temperaments and powers, roused them to think and feel and work as he did.

Take his immediate followers, take that group of boys, or little more than boys, who gathered about him with unquestioning loyalty in the last desperate venture. They were not especially religious. Even Brown's own sons did not adopt his orthodox interpretation of the Bible. But every man of the company had imbibed the spirit of sacrifice, every man was ready to give his life for the cause their leader had preached to them, every man believed that what he said should be done must be done. "They perfectly worshiped the ground the old fellow trod on," said a Southern observer who had no sympathy with them except in the admiration of splendid courage.[46]

Nor was it only over those who came under his immediate command that Brown exercised the magnetism of inspiration and stimulus. After his capture and during his imprisonment he was surrounded by bitter enemies. But they grew to respect him and some apparently to have a personal regard for him. Even when they condemned his cause, they esteemed his spirit of sacrifice and his superb singleness of purpose. In the years before the crisis came he met some of the keenest and most intelligent men in the United States and they saw and felt in him a man of power, a man of will, a man of ideals above and beyond the common average and level of trivial earthliness. "No matter how inconsistent, impossible, and desperate a thing might appear to others, if John Brown said he would do it, he was sure to be believed. His words were never taken for empty bravado," wrote Frederick Douglass.[47] That enthusiasts like Gerrit Smith should be carried away was perhaps natural. But Emerson was not an enthusiast, Thoreau was not, Theodore Parker was not. All these men spoke of Brown as one gifted for some divine purpose beyond mortality. All of them thanked the humble farmer and shepherd for that thrill of exaltation which is one of the greatest forces that can touch the heart. No one will call John A. Andrew an enthusiast. He was a practical man of the world, versed in the hard conduct of everyday affairs. Yet Andrew said: "Whatever might be thought of John Brown's acts, John Brown himself was right."[48]

And the influence of such a man and such a life and such a death flowed out and on beyond the men who obeyed him, beyond the men who met him, to those who never knew him and had hardly even heard of him, to the whole country, to the wide world. The song that carries his name inspired millions throughout the great Civil War, it has inspired millions since, and John Brown's soul and sacrifice were back of the song. That is what Brown meant when he said, "I am worth inconceivably more to hang than for any other purpose." [49] That is what men of his type achieve by their fierce struggle and their bitter self-denial and their ardent sacrifice. They make others, long years after, others who barely know their names and nothing of their history, achieve also some little or mighty sacrifice, accomplish some vast and far-reaching self-denial, that so the world, through all its doubts and complications and perplexities, may be lifted just a little towards ideal felicity. Whatever their limitations, their errors, whatever taint of earthly damage has infected their souls, it may justly be said that "these men, in teaching us how to die, have at the same time taught us how to live." [50]

VII
PHINEAS TAYLOR BARNUM

CHRONOLOGY

Born, Bethel, Connecticut, July 5, 1810.
Married Charity Hallett, November 8, 1829.
Purchased American Museum, 1841.
Engaged Tom Thumb, 1842.
Exhibited in Europe, 1844.
Managed Jenny Lind tour, 1850–1851.
Clock Company failure, 1856.
Wife died, November 19, 1873.
Married Nancy Fish, 1874.
Died, Bridgeport, Connecticut, April 7, 1891.

VII

PHINEAS TAYLOR BARNUM

I

PHINEAS TAYLOR BARNUM! The very sound is com-
pact of a large and common hilarity,

> "Of joy in widest commonalty spread."

Phineas Taylor Barnum! And his wife was Charity
Barnum, and his sister, Minerva Barnum: all in a con-
catenation accordingly, as Tony Lumpkin and Sir
Walter would have it. Barnum! The name itself is
redolent of shows and showmen, and a showman he
was, as his Autobiography abundantly makes manifest, from his youth in the thirties till he died at
eighty, in 1891, the monarch of The Greatest Show
on Earth. So far from feeling disgraced by his calling,
he boasted of it on all possible occasions, appropriate
and inappropriate. "I am 'a showman' by profession,
and all the gilding shall make nothing else of me.
When a man is ashamed of his origin, or gets above his
business, he is a poor devil, who merits the detesta-
tion of all who know him." [1]

Apart from his singular and absorbing business,
Barnum was a good average, you might say, typical,

191

American citizen. He was twice married, had daughters, and was an affectionate husband and father. He says so and others agree with him. The supplement to his Autobiography written by his second wife after his death, shows a genuine tenderness which could have been inspired only by a kindly nature, and gives an amiable picture of the great showman in his home, with a group of grandchildren and great-grandchildren about him.

He was eminently a social creature always, liked people of all sorts, to have them in his house, chat with them, laugh with them, frolic with them. His acquaintance was vast, included everybody. In Europe and America he fraternized with high and low. Samuel Rogers and the Bishop of London jested with him. Mark Twain and Matthew Arnold visited him. He would walk or talk or work or play with whoever happened to be his companion at the moment. "As a host he could not be surpassed," says one who visited him often. "He knew the sources of comfort — what to omit doing, as well as what to do, for a guest. He had the supreme art of making you really free, as if you were in your own house." [2]

As in his human relations, so in his intellectual traits, Barnum was an average man. He was quick, shrewd, immensely keen to grasp the practical bearing of a problem. If he interested himself in any speculative matter, he would clarify it speedily, or let it alone, as not worth clarifying. He was an expert mathematician, at least as concerned dollars and cents. But he had little education and little real interest in abstract questions. It is important to note that, although his business kept him in close contact with all sorts of animals, his Autobiography does not show the faintest trace of scientific curiosity. Neither does it indicate any affection for a single one of the numerous creatures who must have come more or less directly under his observation.

Matters of art did not take any more real hold of him than matters of intellect. It is true, he is careful to inform us that his own taste was much above the Museum. "I myself relished a higher grade of amusement, and I was a frequent attendant at the opera, first-class concerts, lectures, and the like."[3] Also, his admiration for the beauties of nature shows itself in a delicious tirade against those who mar such beauties by hideous advertising. "It is outrageously selfish to destroy the pleasure of thousands, for the sake of a chance of additional gain."[4] But I do not find evidence that either the painting of Botticelli or a quiet walk in the fields afforded him any particular ecstasy.

Barnum's religion was of a good, practical, working quality, rather than of mystical depth. It often appears in queer connections and disappears in queerer. But, after all, in this muddled world whose religion can be consistently counted on? Barnum's was, I am sure, sincere and genuine at bottom. The worth of salvation and the shadow of hell gripped his practical youth and the influence of these things never let go. His little pamphlet on the principles of the Universalist faith shows some reading and a good deal of serious thinking, and he said shrewd and tender things about life and death both. "Of his own death he would not speak," says Mrs. Barnum; "of death in the abstract he said: 'It is a good thing, a beautiful thing, just as much so as life; and it is wrong to grieve about it, and to look on it as an evil.'" [5] As to life and the beliefs back of it, he remarked, with keen insight, "If the fact could be definitely determined, I think it would be discovered that in this 'wide-awake' country there are more persons humbugged by believing too little than too much." [6]

In his relation to the affairs of the community at large Barnum was always an active and a useful citizen. Here again he himself is liberal with information and commendation, but this testimony is amply supported by that of others. He was mayor of his

own city, Bridgeport, and a member of the legislature
of Connecticut, and as such he fought abuses and advocated reforms, and was always a conspicuous and
sometimes a significant figure. He was a candidate
for Congress; but according to his own account
party considerations defeated him. Perhaps the
voters did not wholly relish being represented by a
man whom the world at large could not be persuaded
to take seriously.

General reforms attracted this zealous worker as
well as political. Above all, for many years he
preached — and practised — total abstinence. His
story of his conversion and final abjuring of alcohol
is most edifying. He lost no occasion of lecturing on
the subject, with an abundant and vigorous rhetoric.
"In the course of my life," he says, "I have written
much for newspapers, on various subjects, and always
with earnestness, but in none of these have I felt
so deep an interest as in that of the temperance reform."[7] And again, in his later years: "At my stage
of life I confess to a deeper interest in the noble cause
of temperance than I ever had in the largest audience
ever assembled under canvas."[8]

And he worked and gave as well as talked. As his
wealth grew, he dispensed it with broad and wise
liberality, especially contributing to the develop-

ment and improvement of the city in which he lived. If I cite his own evidence instead of the abundant corroboration of his admirers, it is simply because of its delightful naïveté. "I speak of these things, I trust," he says, "with becoming modesty, and yet with less reluctance than I should do, if my fellow-citizens of Bridgeport had not generally and generously awarded me sometimes, perhaps, more than my meed of praise for my unremitting and earnest efforts to promote whatever would conduce to the growth and improvement of our charming city." [9]

But, though Barnum's avocations and diversions may have been politics and philanthropy and reform, his real life was in his business. From his infancy his thoughts were devoted to making money, to getting a good bargain, even on a small scale. As a child he was given pennies by his grandfather, "to buy raisins and candies, which he always instructed me to solicit from the store-keeper at the 'lowest cash price.'" [10] The boy concentrated all his mental energy on the study of the qualities that would enable him to get and keep. He was born with a natural instinct in such matters: "I usually jump at conclusions, and almost invariably find that my first impressions are correct"; [11] and he improved his natural instincts to a point that made him a phenomenon.

196

Note, however, that the driving force in all this was not the mere money-greed itself. In this side of his nature Barnum was distinctly and thoroughly American. Foreigners are always accusing Americans of idolizing the dollar. They misunderstand. In reality the American man of business cares nothing for the dollar. He has not the miser's passion for accumulating as such. He is just as ready to spend as he is to gain, to fling away the dollars for amusement or benevolence as fast, almost, as they come in, unless retaining them is clearly necessary to get more. What he idolizes is not money, but success; and success in business, in money-making, is the crude, obvious form that appeals to a nation which has not yet wholly grasped the finer issues and interests of life. This was eminently true of Barnum. To call him avaricious or penurious would be absurd. To be sure, we have to discount a little when he says, "You are much mistaken in supposing that I am so ready or anxious to make money. On the contrary, there is but one thing in the world that I desire — that is, tranquillity." [12] But it is certain that, after he had assured himself against want, what he sought was to carry out his projects. Those projects happened to involve money-making, and he made it.

He did not even care greatly for the things that

money gives. He could, and, when it was necessary, he did, live with the utmost simplicity. When money came, he spent, and no doubt enjoyed, being eminently human. Besides, great spending, even personal, was great advertising. But he did not need dollars for luxury any more than for the mere pleasure of possessing them.

I wish there were detailed evidence as to the most important of Barnum's business qualities, that of dealing with men. His relations with them must have been vast and successful, but he himself throws little light upon the question. Now and then, however, there are glimpses of singular tact and aptitude, and I find one observation, from a man who knew him well, that is illuminating: "In the management of business he was both skilful and acute, but what surprised some was the fact that he habitually asked advice of you, whoever you were, on every matter he had in hand that could be disclosed. In this way he got all sorts of opinions, studied their value, and struck such a balance between them as his own judgment led him to think was the correct one." [13] Such methods of procedure go a long way in accounting for a successful career.

It cannot be denied that the most conspicuous feature in Barnum's business activity was the instinct of speculation, of venturesomeness, of taking a chance. Earning was well. Saving was well. But using your brains to make a big profit out of a small investment was far better. "My disposition," he says, "is, and ever was, of a speculative character, and I am never content to engage in any business unless it is of such a nature that my profits may be greatly enhanced by an increase of energy, perseverance, attention to business, tact, etc."[14] In his youth lotteries were much in fashion. They suited him exactly, and he loved to embark in the wild lotteries of others and to invent wilder of his own. Even after he had left the lottery for other fields, the same gambling instinct clung to him. Only he himself used and enjoined upon others that combination of iron restraint with boldness which alone can bring speculation to success.

As to the moral element of such dubious ventures, Barnum's career offers a most interesting study. That he did not mean to delude and defraud is obvious enough. But his infinite delight in Yankee shrewdness often blinded him to the damaging fact that such shrewdness is too apt to mean plain cheats and lies. He was brought up in an atmosphere of petty trickery which he himself analyzes with the keenest insight and his final comment on it is: "Such a school would 'cut eye-teeth,' but if it did not cut conscience, morals, and integrity all up by the roots, it would be because the scholars quit before their education was completed!" [15] He wrote a huge and curious book on "The Humbugs of the World," mixing and confusing all sorts of trifling deceptions, elaborate frauds, and political and religious delusions and hallucinations. His deduction from this study was that mankind liked to be humbugged and always would be, that some humbug was legitimate and delightful, and that precisely such was his.

Humbug or not, it must not be supposed that his success or his wealth was gained without bitter struggle. As he himself sums it up, with his luminous complacency: "A life with the wide contrasts of humble origin and high and honorable success; of most formidable obstacles overcome by courage and constancy; of affluence that had been patiently won, suddenly wrenched away, and triumphantly regained." [16] To tell the story in more detail, he began poor, worked hard, though he hated work, wandered widely. He kept store, he ran nomadic shows, he dabbled in journalism, which landed him in jail, whence he emerged with a gorgeous ovation that tickled his whole soul. By feeding men's wonder with strange sights he gathered a considerable property.

Then he became involved, through what seems incredible carelessness, in an investment that practically ruined him. He took disaster with admirable
equanimity, set to work with energy and independence to reëstablish himself, rejected offers of help,
milked the world's gullibility once more on an even
vaster scale, paid his honest debts, and shone out in
the end far more prosperous than when ruin overtook
him. You could not shake his confidence or his hope.
His Museum was burned and burned again. He
laughed and rebuilt it. Competition beset him. He
laughed and declared that the desire for amusement
was the one passion that was inexhaustible. You
might tap it more and more deeply and never find an
end. He collaborated with various partners and some
suggest that the partners contributed largely to the
enterprise and the success.[17] But Barnum got the
credit — and the fun. At one time he thought he had
got enough and done enough. He would give up and
rest and let others do the work and have the profit.
But nature was too strong, and back he went again,
and kept at it till he died. His last inquiry of his secretary was "what were the receipts yesterday?" and
when told they were good, with the figures, he remarked that they were not up to the receipts of the
Olympia in London.[18]

II

It will not be disputed that the greatest element in Barnum's success was advertising. The rapid development of journalism in the last half of the nineteenth century made it preëminently the age of publicity, and few human beings have ever lived who enjoyed publicity, or understood it, or profited by it, more than Barnum did. He recognized this himself at all times. In 1855 he wrote: "Fully appreciating the powers of the press (to which more than to any other one cause I am indebted for my success in life), I did not fail to invoke the aid of 'printer's ink.'" [19] Twenty years later he declared, "Without printer's ink, I should have been no bigger than Tom Thumb." [20] By repeated, unfailing, unblushing proclamation of the merits of his goods he drew the whole world about him, and so enormous was the force at his command that even he did not appreciate its full capacity. On one occasion he was driven to remark, "I lost a large amount of money that day by not having sufficiently estimated the value of my own advertising." [21]

Every agency of direct, paid publicity was of course set constantly at work with all its resources of flare and glitter. Once convinced that he had something worth public attention, he did not hesitate to arouse that attention by all that printing and painting could devise. In his homely way he says, "Advertising is to a genuine article what manure is to land — it largely increases the product." [22]

But direct methods were the smallest part of the matter. It was the cunning and subtle psychological suggestion of every sort and kind that counted most. Barnum speaks with delight of a sign he saw one day on which was written, "Don't read the other side." Every passerby did read the other side and bought in consequence.[23] It was the ingenuity of such things that charmed him quite as much as their profit. Reporters? "Approachable, democratic in every way, and shrewd, he fairly melted to the interviewer, whom he frequently did not wait for, but sent for." [24] Mystery? Infinite are the uses of mystery. Keep people guessing and you keep them interested. Crowds? They bring other crowds. Only make a man feel that his neighbor wants to enter your door and he will jostle the world to get in himself. Elephants? Big, strange creatures, are n't they? Good advertising anywhere. But if we buy a farm in plain sight from a great railroad and set elephants to ploughing it, what a stir we shall make! Pickpockets? You might think them a nuisance about a show. So they are. But if you catch one and shut him up and tell everybody that a live pickpocket may be seen for a quarter, you will draw fools, and some who are not. Barnum did it.[25] Religion? We have the greatest possible respect for religion. But if a minister attacks our show and we can speak up for ourselves and tell his congregation that he is mistaken and that we are one of the greatest moral influences of the age, well, religion will make as good advertising as anything else — and better.[26]

On the dishonest, the fraudulent side of advertising Barnum is inexhaustible and delightful. The ingenuity of his resource is equaled only by the sophistry of his defense. The fierce and solemn reprehension of the great English magazines as to the first edition of his Autobiography should be read and enjoyed. But, after all, these attacks affected chiefly one or two conspicuous frauds, which Barnum himself in later years did not regard with much pride. Joice Heth, the one hundred and sixty year old nurse of Washington, the Mermaid, and the Woolly Horse were not creditable adventures. Barnum confesses that he lied about the age of Tom Thumb and in the earlier Autobiography (omitted in the later) insists that, so long as Tom was really a dwarf, it made no difference.[27] Exaggerated statements, more or less deliberate misrepresentations, ingenious and far-fetched suggestion had confused the great show-man's conscience to such an extent that, so long as the atmosphere of publicity was rosy, its haziness did not seriously disturb him. Yet when it came to actual business transactions, his substantial honesty seems beyond dispute. The whole history of his dealings with Jenny Lind, told from her side as well as from his, supports this. Moreover, he was firmly convinced of the great principle of advertising, which he never loses an occasion to emphasize: it only pays to adver-tise a good thing. Make the public feel that it has got its money's worth, and you may tell it what you please.

As to the speculative aspect of publicity, the ne-cessity of outlay and the uncertainty of return, Bar-num is most interesting and instructive. No one had studied the intricacies of the subject more thoroughly than he. Yet he admits that, with all his experience, it is impossible to tell what will pay and what will not. " 'The public' is a very strange animal, and al-though a good knowledge of human nature will generally lead a caterer of amusements to hit the people, they are fickle and ofttimes perverse." [28] Nothing pleases him more than to combine adver-tising with practical utility. When he was conveying

Tom Thumb through France, the railroad service proved inconvenient and it was necessary to substitute other forms of transportation. The number of the attendants and the various accessories made a great display of vehicles indispensable. But Barnum consoled himself with the thought that it all helped to create interest. "It was thus the best advertising we could have had, and was really, in many places, our cheapest and in some places, our only mode of getting from point to point." [29]

And always, when he was anxious to inform the world, he believed in spending without limit, even if the gain was not directly visible. A man complained to him once that he had a good article and had advertised it but could not sell it. "How did you advertise?" "I put it in a weekly newspaper three times, and paid a dollar and a half for it." And Barnum's comment was, "Sir, advertising is like learning — 'a little is a dangerous thing.'" [30]

If it was a question of getting himself and his wares before the public, Barnum was perfectly ready to appreciate the value of abuse as well as of commendation. Few men have been more scolded, more criticized, more lavishly and scurrilously ridiculed than he. But his skin was thicker, apparently, than that of his own elephants, and so the world talked about him, he did not much care how it talked. He wrote his book to expose the humbugs of history, and he was quite willing that anybody who wished should expose him. A woman came and tried to make him buy a pamphlet in which she had found fault with his procedure. My dear madam, he said in substance, write what you please: "only have the kindness to say something about me, and then come to me and I will properly estimate the money value of your services to me as an advertising agent." [31] "It's a great thing to be a humbug," he quotes from a kindred spirit, "I've been called so often. It means hitting the public in reality. Anybody who can do so, is sure to be called a humbug by somebody who can't." [32] Again and again he returns to this point: "The object was accomplished and although some people cried out 'humbug,' I had added to the notoriety which I so much wanted and I was satisfied." [33] Finally, in one precious and perfect phrase, he sums up his whole attitude in the matter: "After all, it was a good advertisement for me, as well as for Higginson; and it would have been pretty difficult to serve me up about these times in printer's ink in any form that I should have objected to." [34]

Nor was he satisfied with working through the newspapers, or through the tongues of others, or through a hundred subtle, indirect agencies of every kind. He was always ready to appear before the world in person, to tell it of the merits of his shows and incidentally — and largely — of his own, to talk anywhere and without limit. He assures us of his imperturbable coolness on the platform. You could not upset his equanimity or exhaust his patience. His golden, or brazen, abundance of words was unstinted, whether with tongue or pen. He could talk on any subject, telling stories, quoting authors, making points of all sorts, and always attracting the attention of wider and wider multitudes to the incomparable excellence of the greatest show on earth. And it cannot be denied that he made words serve his purpose with a deftness and facility calculated to increase the distrust of even persons who regard those insinuating agents with the extremest scepticism. He spoke and wrote well, with lucidity and energy, about politics, finance, temperance, general virtue, even religion. That he did not always live up to the high level of his eloquence is of less account, because a verbal standard so lofty would have been beyond the reach of any man. But if you take the words by themselves, they do tell. The little pamphlet in which he, for a wonder concisely, expounds his Universalist beliefs, is a statement of singular vigor and directness.

Do not sentences like these snap and sting? "The force of habit is indeed strong, but this argument overloads it tremendously. . . . If a man cannot will to obey, he cannot sin. He is not a responsible actor. If death does this we are all alike unmanned. There can be neither heaven nor hell; we are not men, but things." [35]

And it is everywhere evident that the man was not going before the public simply from business motives: He loved it. The advertising instinct was bound up in his nature with an extraordinary childlike vanity. You can see it written all over him. A huge, benevolent, inimitable expansiveness radiates from every portrayal of his face and figure. He liked to talk of himself, had a large, shrewd gift of narrating all sorts of adventures in which he was the hero — or the butt, at any rate the significant personage. He boasted of everything, even of his modesty. Of one of his earlier undertakings he says, it "led me into still another field of enterprise which honorably opened to me that notoriety of which in later life I surely have had a surfeit." [36] But if surfeit means enough, it does not appear that the point was ever really reached. With what joy does he record the arrival of the time when "visitors began to say that they would give more to see the proprietor of the Museum than to view the entire collection of curiosities." [37]

And all the vanity, all the love of popular applause, or even abuse, is poured out in the immense, singular document called "Struggles and Triumphs," the huge Autobiography which sets forth so many things that happened and that did not happen and makes the wide world revolve around that jovial heap of kindly egotism. What a book! What a collection of books! For it was revised over and over, and printed and re-printed in half a dozen different forms, all ingeniously adapted to entice dollars from purses fat and lean and ragged and gorgeous. How he did love it, how he thought over it and worked over it, the precious record of his abounding and world-agitating self. Not Henry James could have given more care to the revision of his earlier writings to suit his later glory than did this busy and in a sense illiterate showman. The crude anecdotes, the crowding vulgarisms, of 1855, are *chastened*, to use his own favorite word, in the editions of the seventies, so that they may not profane the transformation from thousands of readers to tens of thousands. Heaven knows there are still enough left. Up to his death he added a yearly chapter, that not one precious fact might be unnoted, and he enjoined upon his disconsolate widow the melancholy completion, which unhappily he could not set down himself.[38]

So from the cradle to the grave his impulse was to keep always before the people. In Mr. Conklin's excellent book about the circus there is a vivid picture of Barnum, showing how he reveled in the opportunity of exhibiting himself to applauding crowds. "Soon after the show began he arrived in an open carriage drawn by two horses, with a coachman and footman in full livery on the box. The whole performance came to a stop while he was driven slowly around the hippodrome track. At intervals he would have the carriage stop, and standing up in it, call out in his squeaky voice, 'I suppose you came to see Barnum, did n't you? Wa-al, I'm Mr. Barnum.'" [39] For fifty years he had been proclaiming through a megaphone to the admiring universe, "I'm Mr. Barnum."

III

THE palliation for all this immense and undeniable vulgar egotism, the excuse which made the world tolerate it and makes those who read about it tolerate it still, was first, the man's benefaction to humanity in public entertainment. Here again no one can state his own merits more emphatically than he does. "Every man's occupation should be beneficial to his fellow-man as well as profitable to himself. All else is vanity and folly." [40] "Men, women and children, who cannot live on gravity alone, need something to satisfy their gayer, lighter moods and hours, and he who ministers to this want is in a business established by the Author of our nature," [41] which is certainly putting the circus under respectable patronage. But that Barnum did labor to amuse mankind as well as to enrich himself cannot be disputed.

As to the quality of the amusement there may be some question. Critics, of what, if he had lived fifty years later, he would have called a highbrow order, are unsparing in their condemnation. If he did not degrade and deprave public taste, he at least appealed to much that was degraded and depraved in it. If he was careful to avoid conflict with the more obvious principles of morality, he at least fed the idly and vulgarly curious with entertainment that tended to crowd all that was fine and noble out of their lives. I should not undertake to determine the truth of this complicated charge, merely pointing out that the reprehensible features of Barnum's shows gradually gave way to what was more wholesome, and that since his time some diversions have evolved at least as objectionable as any invented by him. The interesting thing is his own complete self-complacency in the matter. To his mind all that he offered the public was beneficial and improving in the highest degree

and every shade of the harmful was carefully elimi-
nated. I do not see how this can be urged with more
force than in the concluding words of the 1880 edition of his Autobiography: "When it is evident that
the public, old and young, are not made wiser, better
and happier by the recreation which I provide for
them, my efforts in that direction will cease."

As to the quantity of amusement furnished there
will be less question than as to the quality. "Taken
altogether, I think I can, without egotism, say that I
have amused and instructed more persons than any
other manager who ever lived." [42] So writes this
creature of infinite self-content. And he proceeds to
give figures to prove that in all he had exhibited to
over eighty-two million persons. This, of course, as he
is careful to point out, may include the same visitor
many times. But even so, it is a vast total of human
delight. And while the majority must consist of the
youthful and the uneducated, we know that young
and old, high and low, man and woman, the million-
aire, the scholar, the preacher, all alike meet at the
circus and the menagerie. The child is the pretext,
but the immortal child in all of us is the explanation.
Who has been such a benefactor to children as Barnum, and who like him has teased the child out of the
weary and fretted and forgetful man?

Moreover, we forgive much not only to his faculty of entertaining others, but to his own exuberant delight in what he was doing. Some entertainers are anxious and worried, like the rest of us. They make amusement a business like another, dry and shrink up in a back office, while the huge, mad riot of the world is going on about them. Not so Barnum. It was his riot and his world, and he savored every thrill of its enjoyment as if it were his own. He could himself perform, if necessary, could do sleight-of-hand tricks, or black up and sing negro songs, anything to divert the waiting multitude, if occasion called for it. He could plunge into strange antics, for the mere zest, as when he visited the South of France in vintage-time: "While I was there, desiring a new experience, I myself trod out a half barrel or so with my own naked feet, dancing the while to the sound of a fiddle." [43] But most of all he reveled in the glory of exhibiting glory. He knew it was second-hand, knew it was mere reflection. With a pretty mock-modesty he sometimes tried to shrink into the background. But why? It was Barnum who pulled the wires, Barnum who set these puppets dancing and doing their clever tricks, and all the world knew it, and he was Barnum. Why not enjoy it?

The truth was, he enjoyed everything. Life was a

huge joke, and jokes were the spice that seasoned his whole existence. From the first page of his Autobiography to the last there is a succession of jokes, some clever, some vulgar, some monstrous, but all side-splitting, or so he found them. The taste was inborn, he says, and from his cradle his grandfather and all his family made him the butt of a jest about an inherited mud-patch called Ivy Island. The germ caught in his system and for seventy years he played jokes on all about him and expected them to be played upon him in return. His splendid health, his ever-abounding spirits, all conspired to keep him daily and nightly in the mood of this perpetual frolic.

Note that there is no particular wit or element of intelligence about this fun of Barnum's. Now and then he strikes a happy retort, as when the Bishop of London expressed the assurance, at parting, that they would meet in heaven, and Barnum said, "If your Lordship is there." But in the main it is the un-failing outflow of a vigorous temperament, taking the form of so-called practical jokes, rich with the sugges-tion of a large, luscious, animal felicity, but not es-pecially diverting in the record, and quite often de-generating into dulness.

Also, there were worse elements than dulness. The practical joke, as every one knows, runs too easily

into cruelty, and Barnum's were not exempt from
this feature. Mr. Benton insists that "his most auda-
cious performances and jokes were unqualifiedly
good-humored." [44] So they were in intention, no
doubt; but Barnum himself says of the town where he
passed much of his youth, "A joke was never given up
in Bethel until the very end of it was unraveled," [45]
and we all know what that means. It was immensely
humorous to send forged dispatches on All Fools' Day
to his employees, but the man who was informed that
his native village was in ashes and his own homestead
burned could not have passed a pleasant hour. [46] It
was a rollicking jest that a ticket-taker should be challenged to a duel by an angry student. But "as he expected to be shot, he suffered the greatest mental
agony. About midnight, however, after he had been
sufficiently scared, I brought him the gratifying intelligence that I had succeeded in settling the dispute." [47] Read in cool quiet, these things do not altogether amuse. And I feel still more the callousness
they suggest in Barnum's apparent complete indifference to the semi-humanity or sub-humanity of the
horrible creatures that he often exhibited. One would
think that a nature with a shred of sensitiveness
would have recoiled from the public display of these
monstrosities and the sickening, morbid curiosity

they fostered. Sensitiveness of that kind Barnum had not.

Even worse than the mixture of joke with cruelty is the mixture with dishonesty, because the combination is more easily effected and more insidious. Barnum's preoccupation with this side of the matter is always evident. When, as a boy, he was a clerk in a store and tricked his customers, he remarks that some of them "were vexed, but most of them laughed at the joke." [48] When he has advanced much farther in experience and success, he comforts himself for various odd procedures with the reflection that "the public appears disposed to be amused even when they are conscious of being deceived." [49] The earlier chapters of his elaborate study of "Humbug" are largely given up to a specious apology for his own career. With extreme and far-reaching ingenuity he argues that humbug and swindling are very different matters. With all respect for his cleverness, however, I think the average honest man will hold that humbug in everything even remotely connected with money does mean swindling and nothing else. The peculiarity of humbug is that it is swindling with a sense of humor, of practical joke, in it. This is what makes it tolerable to the American public, and this is just what fascinated Barnum, profitable practical joking. But it may be questioned whether either the precept or the example was of advantage to American youth.

Yet, in spite of all the callousness and all the trickery inherent in the joking habit, there was at the bottom of the jokes, in Barnum's case, a vast and jovial good-nature which you cannot help admiring and liking and enjoying. Tried by the final test of the joker, that of being willing to take a joke on himself, he comes out with an unfailing cheerfulness and a hearty sense of reciprocity which always command respect. He tells innumerable pranks that were played upon him, in full detail and with huge impersonal relish. To be sure, he usually contrives a sequel by which the rash jester is amply repaid. But it must be admitted that he does not hesitate a moment to show himself in a ridiculous light, even when he has been placed there by his own folly. And this is only part of the general winning candor of self-confession, by which, so far as he sees, which perhaps is not to the very bottom, he places his whole heart before the reader of his pages. At times, as is apt to be the case with such candor, he reaches a point of joking self-depreciation that is misleading and might easily tempt the critic to judge him more severely than he deserves. Thus it was that in his later years, after a life of far-extended beneficence, he could say in public,

"Mine is usually a *profitable philanthropy*. I have no desire to be considered much of a philanthropist in any other sense." [50]

When finally analyzed, a good deal of philanthropy brings its profit in one way or another. But few people have had the kindly instinct of spreading and promoting joy more fully than Barnum. He believed that the Americans "with the most universal diffusion of the means of happiness ever known among any people," [51] were unhappy, and he wanted to make them cheerful. He believed in laughter, wanted to make people laugh, and "men who had not laughed for twenty years, or maybe never, held aching sides when it was their good fortune to meet P. T. Barnum in a merry mood." [52] He loved children, above all things loved to make them happy, and did it, and next to becoming like a little child — and Barnum was not unlike one — is there any surer passport to the Kingdom of Heaven? He turned his whole circus parade out of its route to amuse a sick boy who had dreamed for days of seeing it. [53] To be sure, these things sooner or later found their way into the papers and made famous advertising, and the philanthropy was profitable. But the philanthropy was there, just the same, and some men like the profit without it.

So he lived and died, the great showman of the

world, making the world into a show, making a show of everything in it, and all the time himself furnishing the greatest show of all. And he knew it, reveled in it, was as ready to turn himself into laughter as anything else. The glorification of laughter has its weak points, the weakest perhaps being that those who laugh easily are inclined to laugh too much and quite out of place. But in the world as it is to-day many of us might laugh, or smile, a little more, and Barnum at least did his part toward diffusing the habit.

It is true that at moments, in keen and sincere recollection of his religious training, he tried to pull a long face and emphasize the solemn trumpet tone of the Koran sentence, "The heavens and the earth, think ye that we have created them to be a jest?" With his inimitable verbal facility he could reproduce this tone, as he could many others: "The endless ages of immortal life are not given to sit on a flower-bed and sing and play harps, but for the endless development of immortal souls." [14] But this was not his natural vein, was not in the essential temper of his spirit. If he lingers in history at all, or in the memory of his American fellow countrymen, whom he amused so vastly, it will be as a trifling bubble of riotous and somewhat vulgar laughter on the stream of the Infinite Illusion.

VIII
BENJAMIN FRANKLIN BUTLER

CHRONOLOGY

Born, Deerfield, New Hampshire, November 5, 1818.
Removed to Lowell, 1828.
Graduated at Waterville College, Maine, 1838.
Admitted to Bar, 1840.
Married Sarah Hildreth, May 16, 1844.
Supported Breckinridge in 1860.
Major-General of Volunteers, May, 1861.
Commanded in New Orleans, 1862.
Commanded in Virginia, 1864.
Relieved from command, January, 1865.
Active in politics, 1866–1884.
Prominent in impeachment of Andrew Johnson, 1868.
Wife died, 1877.
Governor of Massachusetts, 1883.
Died, Washington, D.C., January 11, 1893.

VIII
BENJAMIN FRANKLIN BUTLER

I

And still I am looking for a real, live rascal, one who knows and confesses himself to be such, and boasts of it, who does not dodge and shift and palter and whip the devil round the stump, to whom principle is nothing, conscience is nothing, God is nothing, and self and pleasure and success are all. If I could find him, he should have first place among all these palely damaged, but not completely damned souls. I have not found him yet and he is certainly not General Benjamin Franklin Butler. On the contrary, it was always Butler's strenuous assertion, and very likely conviction, that his aims were the highest and his acts not far behind them. As he aptly expressed it, of one particular phase, "I have done nothing but good and that *continually.*" [1]

But however contented Butler might be with his own virtue, his enemies thought him a rascal of the worst description, and he had hosts of them, though he had also loyal and devoted friends. His vigorous, impetuous, insolent temper seemed to revel in hostility and to think it fun to be hated. He himself believed that he was disliked because he was always with the under-dog in a fight,[2] though there were those who insinuated that he cheered on the under-dog, but was not so ready to haul off the upper one. At any rate, he made enemies from the start and kept on making them. As a young lawyer in Lowell and Massachusetts legislator in the forties and fifties, he became obnoxious to those in position and power by speaking and arguing, less often it was said by voting, for radical measures, and by pleading causes that did not always deserve to be successful, though he often made them so. He was forty-two when the Civil War came, and he plunged into it with eagerness having long devoted himself to the study and practice of military matters. As a major-general of volunteers in Louisiana and Virginia he grew to be an object of peculiar loathing to the Southerners. He also created antagonism in the executive of his own state and in powerful elements of the regular army and navy and of the government. It may have been fun, but it was disastrous; and he was relegated to Lowell before the close of the war. In later years he made innumerable enemies in both political parties, by shifting from one to the other. Decorous newspapers decried him, what is called society eschewed him, professors and well-groomed people generally detested him. When, after repeated efforts, he won the governorship of Massachusetts, in 1883, Harvard College, for the first time in its history refused him the degree of doctor of laws. From 1884, when he received a presidential nomination, till his death in 1893, he avoided politics, practised his profession zealously and profitably, and laughed at his enemies. All the same, they have made terrible havoc with his reputation ever since, and the efforts of his friends to have his statue erected in the grounds of the Massachusetts State House led only to bitter and repeated denunciations of his name and memory, which the warmest arguments of his grandchildren hardly sufficed to repel.

The whole question of Butler's character and his picturesque career is so tangled and varied and complicated that a dogmatic presentation of it is impossible, at least for me. But by summing up first the substance of the attacks made upon him, then the ardent advocacy of his friends, and finally letting the man depict himself at full length before us, a display which was never repugnant to him, I think a fairly close and complete impression may be obtained. Let us see, then, first what his enemies said of him, as a lawyer, as a soldier, as a politician, as a financier.

His ability in legal matters is not seriously contested. It was perhaps rather of the surface order, more apt at sudden turns and tricky surprises than at profound logical argument. But beyond question his clients believed in him and his adversaries dreaded him, dreaded his infinite resource and his terrible tongue. According to the verdict of Senator Chandler, he was "as able a member of the profession as the country contains, and certainly the most remarkable one." [3] Yet listen to those pestilent enemies through the voice of George F. Hoar: "Quiet and modest men who had the confidence of the courts and juries used to win verdicts from him in fairly even cases. . . . He was seldom content to try a simple case in a simple way. So that, while he succeeded in some desperate cases, he threw away a good many which with wise management he might have gained." [4]

And now the soldier. Here there are two Butlers, the general in the field and the administrator. As to the administrator his compatriots north of Mason and Dixon's line are less disposed to quarrel. His methods of government were severe, as in the execution of Mumford in New Orleans, rough sometimes to the point of brutality, and, as in the case of Chaplain Hudson, they do not always seem to have been exempt from personal spite; but every one admits that they were immensely effective. Speed and energy of performance were closely attendant upon a singular fertility and shrewdness of resource in conception. The control of New Orleans, the control of eastern Virginia, the control of riotous New York, were not child's play, and Butler achieved them. The enemies who reviled and maligned him here were the enemies of the country and generally speaking such abuse is not regarded as discrediting a commanding officer. But in Butler's case it is so extreme and so well-directed that it is difficult to pass it over altogether. Take the notorious order which put a stop to the impertinence of the Southern women by proclaiming that, if they did not behave themselves, they were liable to be treated as women of the town. The remark of Fiske, that "its wretched author" could not have "understood in the smallest degree the feelings of gentlemen," [5] is exaggerated. But — well, the order was not exactly nice: it is impossible to imagine Grant, or even Sherman issuing it; Napoleon might have.

As to Butler the campaigner, the controversies are hot and hopeless. In such a thorny professional subject a layman can hardly have an opinion. Some deny the general's courage, many his ability. Halleck speaks of "his total unfitness to command in the field, and his general quarrelsome character." [6] W. F. Smith called him "as helpless as a child on the field of battle and as visionary as an opium-eater in council." [7] But Halleck and Smith were both liars, in Butler's opinion; in any event, they detested him. Meigs, who was specially detailed to report on Butler's field command, says "he has not experience and training to enable him to direct and control movements in battle." [8] And Sherman wrote, "He always struck me as a mighty man of words, but little in deeds of personal valor." [9] It must at least be said that Butler accomplished nothing of notable consequence in a military way. New Orleans was taken, but the navy claimed the victory. Petersburg was not taken, Fort Fisher was not taken. There were plenty of excuses in every case. The general's friends assert that he was not supported and blame the jealousy of West Point. But the fact remains. "The test of merit in my profession, with the people, is success," said Albert Sidney Johnston; "it is a hard rule, but I think it right." [10] Success is a lamentable and often a cruel criterion; but it is difficult to establish any other, and it is the one that posterity most frequently applies.

In politics it would seem that Butler was more at home than on the battle-field; yet his enemies hound him here also, perhaps even more implacably. They deny that he was ever associated with any large constructive effort of permanent value. They accuse him of taking advantage of popular passions and sensational situations, like the Tewksbury scandal. His name is largely connected with measures of a distinctly unsavory character, the Sanborn contracts, the Salary Grab, the issue of greenbacks, the attempt to pay war debts in a depreciated currency. Above all, it is charged that he changed his party allegiances to suit his personal convenience, and that no man was more zealous to use political power for the aggrandizement of himself and his friends. "Butler . . . was a spoilsman of the lowest order," says Mr. Rhodes.[11]

It is in this point of spoils, of financial corruption and dishonesty, that the charges against Butler are most clinging and most persistent. They were made fiercely, obstinately, and definitely at all times in his career, and perhaps they are summed up with most bitterness in Mr. Moorfield Storey's pamphlet, "The Record of Benjamin F. Butler." Mr. Storey's charges are mainly accepted by Mr. Rhodes, but, as in the case of the similar attack on Blaine, a spirit of intense partisanship is manifest in them, and some at least of Mr. Storey's allegations are energetically disputed by Butler's grandchildren, Mr. Adelbert Ames and Mrs. Marshall. Outside of the war period the charge most frequently brought is that of malversation of funds in connection with the Soldiers' Home; yet, complicated as the affair was, it seems as if we should give some weight to the assertion of the judge before whom it was tried, that "nothing had occurred in the testimony which reflected in the slightest degree upon the integrity or honesty or upright conduct of anybody who was concerned or had at any time been concerned in the transactions." [12]

But it was the commercial dealings connected with his name during the war that laid the greatest burden on Butler's reputation for honesty. While he was governing New Orleans and again in eastern Virginia, an enormous speculative trade was carried on with the enemy. The government authorized this trade under strict regulations, for the sake of getting the cotton. But private individuals were supposed to profit vastly and to violate the regulations with no thought for anything but their own personal plunder. And many who were close to Butler, including his own brother and his brother-in-law, had peculiarly favorable opportunities. Observers like Denison, who were by no means unfriendly to Butler, condemned the trade in general and complained of his relation to those concerned in it. It is true that Mr. Rhodes, who criticizes Butler severely, admits that there is no absolute proof against him.[13] "He is such a *smart* man," says Denison, "that it would, in any case, be difficult to discover what he wished to conceal." [14] It is true that the extreme Southern accusations of theft, as to silver for instance, are utterly unfounded, though there appears to have been a lack of delicacy in the purchase of valuables at low prices wrung from the starved necessity of those who had suffered by the war. But, while nothing can be actually proved, the taint followed Butler at New Orleans and at Norfolk both. Wherever he was, there was the disreputable trade. And no other officer of his rank, north or south, is seriously accused of such transactions. It would be absurd even to suggest them with Grant or Sherman.

Whatever Butler's personal concern with the matter, there was no excuse for the crowd he had about him. All his life he was as loyal in sticking to his friends as he was indiscreet in the choice of them. What his enemies thought of his surroundings it is unnecessary to indicate. More interesting are the repeated suggestions and admonitions of his supporters, those who believed in him and those who profited by him. One of them quoted Secretary Chase as saying, "Why will General Butler allow his friends to be so loaded, so embarrassed with his commercial connections?" and advises extreme caution.[15] And the tone of the letters he receives is too often significant, implying an attitude in financial and other matters to say the least far from delicate.

But the testimony which is to me most striking is that of the witness who followed General Butler's career in all its phases with tender and passionate solicitude and whose vision was in many respects as keen as her sympathy was profound, I mean his wife. I shall have much more to say about her later; but on this matter of the general's financial connections her evidence is immensely impressive. To begin with, in the early days of the war she lays her finger on the essential weakness (italics mine); "Beside the fond devotion of a wife, there is still the same responsibility felt by me for whatever you may do, as there was years ago when you laid your head on my lap, and prayed me to look kindly and lovingly into your face. I saw then what I have since seen in Paul, but not in the other children, *peculiarities easily wrought upon*, and dangerous from their very simplicity."[16] When the complications increase, she pleads and entreats for prudence and common-sense: "I would not have men holding places or trading in my Department to any great extent whom I could not trust at home. They will bring discredit that will worry you hereafter."[17] And the note of overwhelming tragedy in her outcry as to that fatal brother is more poignant than the blow of any enemy: "Is it not enough to make one mad that [after the] two years of agony which I have borne, and after I had proved to him that Jackson was the cause of his failure at Fortress Monroe, yet again that he should bestow all power and give all confidence once more, to have his reputation assailed, and the power he has and might yet gain, slip from his grasp and crumble to nothing?"[18] Is more needed to show that Butler kept about him a class of persons that would damage any man?

To sum up this chapter of enemies, my impression is that during the greater part of his career Butler managed to win the dislike and mistrust of a large majority of those who think themselves the better class of people: not by any means of all, as will be shown later, but of a considerable majority. You may belittle these people as much as you please. You may sneer at them and snub them. You may mock at Harvard College and the New York "Nation" and the Boston "Transcript." You may proclaim yourself entirely contented with the laudation of the illiterate and the adoration of the unclean. You may point out that the Scribes and Pharisees thought themselves the better class, while your followers freely pronounce that "your name, like Jesus of Nazareth, will stand chiseled in the principles of justice and righteousness as long as God shall revolve this world." [19] Nevertheless, that contemptible better class dominates history, guides education, and controls the opinion of generations to come. The severe judgment of Mr. Storey and Mr. Rhodes represents the judgment of thousands and tends to produce the judgment of millions. And such a weight of odium however right or wrong, well or ill founded, makes a prodigious burden for a man's memory to struggle against through the progress of the years.

II

Now to consider the very extensive testimony in favor of General Butler. To begin with, a word should be said about the labors of his granddaughter Mrs. Marshall. This lady has collected in five huge volumes the correspondence bearing upon the general's life through the war period. It is hard to say enough about the thoroughness and the wide candor with which this task has been accomplished. Mrs. Marshall could not better prove her own complete confidence in her grandfather's integrity and nobility than by gathering and printing, as she has done, the bitterest attacks of his enemies as well as the defence of his friends. So far as my examination goes, she has performed this duty with impartiality. She has indeed, omitted the quotation marks which give all the sting to the bitter "Excellency" letter to Governor Andrew. But in doing this she no doubt followed Parton's theory that those marks were a mistake of the copyist,[20] though such an absurd idea seems to be completely disproved by Butler's own defence of them.[21] If the absolute devotion of his grandchildren could clear a man's memory, Butler's would be stainless.

From Mrs. Marshall's volumes and from other sources we may gather first the friendly evidence of Butler's avowed enemies, and some of them are by no means sparing of it. There were even Southerners who had a good word for him, men and women whom he helped in sore need and who did not hesitate to acknowledge it.[22] I have spoken of the praise of his military administration, in spite of its severity, and those, like Denison, who had condemned his commercial transactions most harshly, were eager to have him back, when they saw the inefficiency that followed his departure from New Orleans.[23] Men like Stanton, who frowned upon his financial reputation, warmly recognized his ability in other directions. Men like

Bowles, who fought him politically, felt his social charm and acknowledged him to be a good fellow, though they thought him a bad citizen.[24]

Butler's relation to the two most prominent personages on the Northern side during the war are profoundly interesting to study. It is clear that in the early days Lincoln was much impressed by his brilliancy and activity. Butler believed that Lincoln was inclined to support him and even asserts that in 1863 the president offered him Grant's command.[25] With his broad political vision Lincoln undoubtedly appreciated the value of Butler's popularity with certain classes all over the country and was willing to make allowance for it. At the same time, against the various presidential compliments that Butler quotes one ought to set Lincoln's remark, when Hay suggested that Butler might be the most dangerous man in the army: "Yes, he is like Jim Jett's brother. Jim used to say that his brother was the damnedest scoundrel that ever lived, but in the infinite mercy of Providence he was also the damnedest fool." [26] As to Grant, the tangle of his feelings in regard to his brilliant subordinate is almost impossible to unravel. First he asked to have him removed. Then he kept him. Then he finally got rid of him, with some severe criticism. Yet, after the war, he toned the criticism down, and said to Young: "I like Butler, and have always found him not only, as all the world knows, a man of great ability; but a patriotic man, and a man of courage, honor, and sincere convictions." [27] The ill-disposed have assumed that Butler had some hold over Grant; [28] at any rate, there are Grant's own words, whatever interpretation you may put upon them. Perhaps I may sum up this attempt to get at the kindly feeling of those who were more or less opposed to Butler by referring to the eulogy of C. A. Dana, who fought him on numerous occasions, but who declared that "for the last quarter of a century at least Benjamin Franklin Butler has stood out as the most original, the most American, and the most picturesque character in our public life," adding that "his intellectual resources were marvelous, his mind naturally adhered to the cause of the poor and the weak, . . . he was no pretender and no hypocrite." [29]

Passing now to the praise of Butler by his friends, it must be admitted that the impression above indicated of a certain lack of discrimination in the choice of these is often painfully emphasized. Too many of the letters from enthusiastic admirers, printed by Mrs. Marshall, like that containing the somewhat profane comparison quoted above, bear unfavorably upon the recipient as well as upon the writer; and one is sometimes tempted to reverse the well-known remark of a supporter of Cleveland: "We love him for the enemies he has made." One eager follower proclaims: "You stand well generally, are well spoken of by the middle class, in the cars, in the barrooms, at the corners, etc., as 'the right man in the right place.'"[30] The compliment might perhaps be regarded as two edged. On the other hand, there is a long list of men of the highest standing in the community and of unimpeachable character, whose praise, bestowed at different times and on different occasions, might be urged as affording satisfactory credentials for any man. Salmon P. Chase, Horace Greeley, Henry Wilson, Wendell Phillips, Charles Sumner, William Lloyd Garrison — all these spoke well of Butler, some of them with enthusiasm, and his friends can hardly be blamed for quoting such testimonials with complacency.

So far we have been dealing with Butler as a public man. The evidence of those who knew him in private life is even more favorable. It is certain that he was kindly, helpful, and generous to the poor and needy, and gave money largely without any thought of return. In social relations those most hostile to him admit that he could be charming. When he dropped politics, his easy gayety, his quick wit, his cordial manner, made him delightful to meet and profitable to converse with. One of the most agreeable pictures of his domestic life is afforded in a letter written by a lady well known in New England for her literary gifts and her estimable character, who visited intimately in the Butler family and was acquainted with all its members: "In his own home I was always struck by his simplicity and frank uprightness. Perhaps you will smile when I say I thought him *single-minded.* He had a contempt for everything mean and small, pity for the suffering, and no pity for the pretender. He had strong likes and dislikes and prejudices, and did not hesitate to show them. He had perfect confidence in his wife, consulted her constantly, he adored his children. . . . I think slander never attacked him in his domestic relations, he was never willing to see women lobbyists, and a woman never came into his private office or saw him alone. He had a reverence for women; and no mother ever had a more devoted son." [31]

But by far the most interesting witness to Butler's good qualities and attractions is the one whom I have already slightly suggested, but whose testimony is quite inexhaustible in significance, his wife. Her numerous letters, as printed by Mrs. Marshall, form a most curious human document in themselves, and, as illustrating her husband, they are beyond price. She was a remarkable woman, and I wish I were writing a portrait of her instead of him. Her energy and ambition and her love of poetry led her to the stage in early life and it was from there that Butler married her. The love of poetry stayed by her, and she quotes Shakespeare as if she knew him by heart. From him perhaps she drew her extraordinarily clear-sighted analysis of herself and those about her. I must quote one general passage out of many, to show what the depth and force of this analysis was: "I do not live like other people, I am confident. I began life entirely different from those I knew. I am as far apart from them now as then. . . . In every fibre of me is woven a romance that will die when I am dead, and not till then. . . . It is not the school-girl fever, that must find an object, make a match, and then is commonplace forever. But a love of beauty, of art, even where it is not cultivated, an instinctive love for it in every form, in books, painting, poetry, and music. . . . There is a deep and keen sensibility in my nature that time does not deaden, I think it only intensifies." [32]

It is easy to imagine the interest of this analytical light thrown upon a career and a spirit like Butler's. The personal relation between the two is absorbing in its charm. The wife seems to fling the great world aside and all his activity in it and concentrate all human life in the beating of their two hearts. Jealousy? Oh, yes, she feels jealousy. When he makes one of his not over-delicate jokes about getting a housekeeper, blonde or brunette, she replies: "I see you have not received my letters, or this matter of housekeepers would not be presented either for blondes or brunettes." [33] Anxiety? Oh, the poignant sting of anxiety! "You, that have time for all the petty details in that obscure spot, can you not find time to answer this one question to your wife? Oh, God! have mercy on me and let me be still." [34] Longing? The intense, burning, devouring solicitude of absence? How she knows it! "Say there shall yet be a time for me, apart from ambitious struggle, which is but dust and ashes, hold me to you with care, as a mother would her sick child, kiss me, love me, and forbid me to die of anguish." [35]

Yet, though all the ambitious struggle may be dust and ashes, she enters into it every moment, with the keen passion of self-forgetful love. It is a delight to watch the intertwisted threads of her remote, world-excluding tenderness and her large zeal to have him make his deserved place in the affairs of men. She advises him as to friends and as to enemies, as to commercial transactions and as to the movement of armies, she analyzes his situation and suggests how to improve it and how to get out of it. When conspiracy threatens and jealousy undermines, she warns and cautions: "Remember still that your most dangerous enemies are not among the rebels. You must not have further trouble with the army officers, — if the provocation is ever so bitter, if it is possible to avoid it. They can strike the heaviest, for they strike in a body." [86] She penetrates the design of battles and the causes of defeat, understands campaigns, military as well as political, or thinks she does. At least she darted keen shafts of vision into the darker secrets of the hearts of men.

And the distinguished lady whom I have cited above as to Butler's family life assumes that because such a woman as this loved her husband with her whole soul, he must be wholly worth loving, could not possibly be what Butler's enemies represented him. Alas, we have already studied Margaret Arnold and Theodosia Burr, spirits as keen and noble as Mrs. Butler, who loved as much and admired as thoroughly, and we have not been able to accept their certificates of character as absolutely unexceptionable. But whether we agree with her estimate or not, no one can resist the fascination of seeing that wide planetary career reflected in the troubled ocean of her tenderness. Whatever secret reserves her acute insight may have made, no one could express more confidence in her husband's power and possible fortune than she: "I do not often praise you, but it is my firm belief that there is but *one man* now known to the people who can save this country in its present critical state from utter loss and confusion irremediable; and that is yourself."[37] In short, behind all the passion, and all the desire, and all the wide, tireless urgency, one cannot help imagining the shadowy grandiose figure of Lady Macbeth, murmuring such words as these: "The death of General Williams has nerved me like steel. Would I were a man. I am stronger in the hour of danger, for then I forget myself and woman's cares, and feel all the high enthusiasm that leads to deeds of fame, and for this reason it is better I should be with you. I could never pull you back from what I thought it your duty to do, but should urge you forward, and help, with all the wit I have."[38] What a wife! And, oh, what a woman!

III

To sum up and complete these portrayals by enemies and friends, we will endeavor to let the general portray himself, an endeavor in which he offers us unlimited assistance, not only in the thousand vast pages of "Butler's Book," but in the endless collection of his letters and speeches of all kinds. Many people have praised him, but it required his own genius to give the fine, discriminating touches, and, alas, he has condemned himself in a fashion to delight his enemies, if not to satisfy them. Again and again I am reminded of his own remark as to some of Johnson's utterances: "If Andrew Johnson never committed any other offence — if we knew nothing of him save from this avowal — we should have a full picture of his mind and heart, painted in colors of living light, so that no man will ever mistake his mental and moral lineaments hereafter." [39] I need not explain that I am well aware of the possibilities of treachery in such an exposure as I am undertaking. The greatest cruelty to a man often is to quote him. I can only say that I try to represent the general as, after months of study and investigation, he actually seems to me.

To some extent a man reveals himself in his outward appearance, and those who have formed a pretty definite estimate of Butler's character will probably find some reflection of it in the portraits of his later life: the rotund, heavy, ungainly figure, the heavily drooping cheeks, the heavily drooping eyelids, with the well-known defect of vision, the drooping mustache and scanty locks, the domed forehead, radiant of benevolence. And this is age. But such likenesses as that on page 79 of "Butler's Book" suggest that the youth was not unlike the grown man. Butler himself gives a vivid description of his childhood, but one cannot help suspecting that it is slightly idealized. The boy of ten who looked down upon the little town of Lowell and said to himself: "Here is to be my home; these people are to be my people, and I must prepare myself to take care of those who are my own in old age and to do such service as I may to these people," [40] would appear rather to be a boy in a book.

Butler's account of his education at Waterville, Maine, and elsewhere is piquant and interesting and his account of his intelligence is even more so. The education was perhaps not very profound, but was certainly discursive. "I suppose that General Butler knows more about more subjects than any other man in this country," declares an enthusiastic admirer. [41] More specific and even more impressive is the general's own summary in his book of the vast range of topics that he was led to investigate in his practice; and his solidly retentive memory enabled him to appear at any rate superficially familiar with many things that the ordinary man is not expected to know anything about. His intellect may not have gone very deep, but it was surprisingly quick and active.

In those matters in which intellect should be most profitably applied, that is, religion and God, Butler is always interesting to follow, but his attitude is not easy to elucidate. He had been well trained in the Bible and his ready memory kept bits of scripture often on his lips. He was profuse in references to our Holy Religion, to "Him who died for all," [42] etc., though such references were not always in the best of taste, as when he said of unreliable products of the Harvard Medical School: "Every institution has bad men in it and every institution has good ones. When Christ, aided by Omniscience, too, chose twelve disciples, he chose one who had a devil. I don't believe the Harvard Medical School averages better than that." [43] As to actual belief, we can only take the general's own word, written in the utmost confidence to his wife: "If I *could* believe, I would become a member of the church, but alas! I have n't faith You may have." [44]

If he had n't faith in things divine, he was not much better supplied with it as regards humanity. He was far too apt to impute low, mean motives for actions that were at least susceptible of being ascribed to a higher source, and he did not sufficiently realize that such imputations have a deadly way of recoiling upon the imputer. He was too ready to fling about terms like liar and thief. To be sure, he insists that he did not use such words except when they were "the only ones that ought to be used." [45] But we never know; and when a man believes he is doing his best and you abuse him, he is inclined to pay you back. I think so often of Butler's own sentence: "When a man calls everybody a liar, he is like the man who said that every man in the town was drunk, for they all seemed to him to stagger." [46]

Disbelief in individuals, however, is perfectly compatible with a belief in the race, at any rate with love and pity for it, and above all a desire to help. Butler's merits in this direction must be recognized, and others besides himself insist upon them, though his own insistence could perhaps at times be dispensed with, and his enemies urge that here, as elsewhere, it is a little difficult to distinguish words from deeds. He did proclaim loudly his sympathy with labor, though labor asserted that he sometimes failed it at a pinch. [47] He did perform distinct services for the negro, independent of putting into circulation the famous phrase "contraband of war." And as to mitigating the fate of prisoners, we should not overlook General Schaff's remark: "It is only due to Butler to say that no man,

North or South, did more, not one even approached him, in persistent endeavor to effect exchange and thereby save thousands of lives." [48]

Much more significant than this general philanthropy, however, is Butler's kindness to individuals. Here also he is himself a not unwilling source of information. But there seems plenty of evidence of generosity and charity which looked for no reward and which well bore out the phrase I have before quoted: "God made me in only one way. I must be always with the under-dog in the fight. I can't help it; I can't change, and upon the whole I don't want to." [49]

And if he was kind to outsiders and strangers, there can be no question about his devotion and tenderness to his family. The charming testimony I introduced earlier is wholly borne out by his own letters to his children, which indicate thorough sympathy with their pursuits and attention to their interests. As for his wife, I have shown her side of the relation; I could fill pages with the analysis of his, and the delicate and instructive response and interaction between them. When she mourns, he cheers her; when she frets, he soothes her; when she advises, he listens to her — respectfully, and often complies; when she cries out for love, he gives it to her, gives it cordially, heartily — and yet, and yet, the tone is a little too much that of one humoring a child, and so she feels it. He loved her, oh, yes, he loved her. But, as she herself says, "Ah me! there is such a wide difference between man's thought and woman's," [50] and God knows, a husband's love is a pitiful thing.

For he has a thousand great affairs to attend to besides loving. He must be a lawyer, a governor, a soldier, a hero, a patriot. The desire and the achievement of all this filled Butler's life, and he portrays them with his usual abundance. His vigor, his energy, his inexhaustible resource are astounding. It is said that in youth he was slight and delicate. If so, he largely overcame his weakness, and his health of body and of spirit was almost unfailing. In spite of all his failures and all his difficulties, the moments of discouragement appear rarely, even in his most confidential letters. He was full of aspiration, full of hope, full of confidence. Patriotism? Well, if you believe him, and I think he believed himself, he was ready to sacrifice everything for his country: "I would even take myself away rather than to do anything which would weaken by one ounce the strength with which the administration should strangle this rebellion." [51] Ambition? Ah, this is a more delicate matter. Those about Butler, his many admirers all over the country, seemed to look to him as the only man who could save it; how? By legal and constitutional means, no doubt, if possible. But, if this was not possible, let him save it by the sword, and in the chaos that would ensue the chances were infinite. How far Butler himself reflected on these chances, it is difficult to say. But that he did reflect on them somewhat is suggested by one priceless bit of intimate confidence, addressed to that wife who was ever on the watch to tease great thoughts out of him, if she did not herself put them in (italics mine): "It is coming — a 'Military Dictator.' God grant the man may be one of power and administrative capacity. Let it come — the man has not developed himself yet — but he will — in the field too, before long. The day of small expedients and small men is getting by. *Well, an empire is the repose as it is the ripeness of nations.*" [52]

Unfortunately these large hopes and soaring thoughts were disfigured by a distressing amount of petty vanity. There was vanity of display, the flying of a flag over the hotel where the governor stayed, the exhibition of showy uniforms and pompous formality. [53] There was the sense and the assertion of self-importance and consequence: if my plans had been followed, if my ideas had been adopted, the outcome would have been so different! This was applied indiscriminately, to South as well as North. "Jefferson

Davis could have, and if I had been at his elbow, as he once desired that I should be, would have attended divine service in his own pew in the church at Washington as President of the Confederacy." [54] "Pardon these suggestions, but I am getting a little nervous with the depletion of our line, and the thought of what I would do were I Lee." [55] One sighs over the abyss of regret that must open before the South, when it thinks of what would have happened if it had had Benjamin F. Butler in the place of Robert E. Lee. Fortunately the North was saved from having this added disadvantage to contend with. What it would have meant may be best appreciated from the colossal remark of Butler himself, which is of course not to be taken too seriously, but just seriously enough: "At any rate, when he [Butler] was there, they had no enemy around the capital. When he was away, the enemy got there. I don't mean to say that those two things had any relation to each other; but it was so." [56]

This element of vanity, which it is always difficult to reconcile with fundamental greatness, is too often present in Butler's defence of himself against his enemies and in his statement of his own achievement. Law? "They say I am sharp. Of course I am sharp. It is only when they cannot imitate it that they complain of my sharpness." [57] Politics? "They all agree, so far as I know, that I have ability enough [to be governor]—plenty of ability—too much. He can do great wrong, that is why it is n't best to have him. But I say that a man that cannot do wrong cannot do much right." [58] War? It would be hopeless to attempt to summarize the vast abundance of the general's self-commendation in this line, but he has done it himself, as well as it can be done, on the concluding page of his Book: "If any general officer, with the same means, did more in the war for the life of the nation, I congratulate him most heartily, but I would like to see his list." [59] In all this magnificent rehearsal there is too much insistence upon what *would* have been done. If due support had been given, if West Point had not thwarted, if this man had not delayed, and another man lied, and another been jealous, what grand results would have been accomplished! But history has trouble enough to chronicle the things that did happen, without stirring up the huge chaos of things that did not.

And worse even than the vanity in Butler's attitude toward his critics and enemies is the low insolence and vilification, which, when so fierce and so constant, indicate something more than mere tone, an essential spiritual lack and taint and damage. Butler's friends say that it was a matter of mere outspokenness, that he was a frank, direct man, who hated red tape and formality and said what he thought. But a man may be frank without being brutal and direct without being scurrilous. Again, it is urged that allowance must be made for his humor. He had undoubtedly a shrewd, coarse wit, which was often misunderstood and got him into trouble. But neither frankness nor humor can excuse or palliate the excesses of that terrible rough tongue. Take the whole correspondence with Governor Andrew at the beginning of the war. Both sides may have made mistakes and shown temper; but Andrew's is the temper of a gentleman, Butler's — is not. Take the unspeakable insubordinate insolence of the farewell to his army, when he was relieved, which even Parton deplores. "I have refused to order the useless sacrifice of the lives of such soldiers, and I am relieved from your command."[60] Take the hideous remark about the New Orleans women, who turned their backs upon the Northerners: "Those women evidently know which end of them looks best."[61] Take the lavish bestowal of bitter epithets upon those who had offended him. Badeau is "the French for 'dirty water.'"[62] Halleck is "a lying, treacherous, hypocritical scoundrel, with no moral sense."[63] Porter is "a reckless, con-

253

sciousless [*sic*], impudent liar." [64]   And so on *ad in-finitum*. The man who indulges perpetually in this sort of thing is more damaged by it than is any one whom he attacks. And the unavoidable implication is that he is judging others by the standard of him-self.

Whereas I am inclined to think that Butler judged others seriously very little, and himself hardly at all. I have studied his huge prolixity with the utmost care for any evidence of self-examination and I find almost none. When he rarely attempts anything of the sort, it is apt to result as follows: "All that I am, all that I am to be, I am now. In fact, it may be that this thing existence or being called I, elevated or de-pressed, may be expanded or compressed thereby, but not to the consciousness of I. Therefore the fu-ture is here, for it can bring to me fears none, hopes few, and expectations from it none." [65] How far, far different from the cool, quiet, subtle touch which that delightful wife is always ready to lay upon her own heart and upon his. And this lack of self-analysis must be taken into account in any general discussion of Butler's aims and motives. Certain things sounded well to say, and he said them. Of course he meant them. Why should n't he mean them? At any rate, just as much as others did. What was the use of plunging and floundering in a vague spiritual chaos to find out what a man meant? In such a chaos I know that I at least have floundered, in the endeavor to find solid bottom in the depths of this complicated soul, and I am forced at last to leave the question of Butler's sincerity between himself and God, with the suspicion that the divine perspicacity has seldom been more severely taxed.

IV

What is certain is, that, however it may have been with thoughts, Butler was a master of words. And I do not mean to say that words were the whole of him: he had many striking and significant qualities besides the power of expression. But words were the worst and the best, and I think his gifts in this direction accounted largely for his prominences and for what success he had. It is said he had not the natural graces of oratory. Perhaps not; but he understood an audience, knew how to take advantage of every favorable turn, or every weak point in the argument of an adversary. He was always at his ease, always ready, never discomfited by any awe or excess of reverence. Moreover, he had an illimitable flow of language. And this is even more evident in his writing than in his speaking. When you probe his documents to the very bot-

tom, you may not find any great coherence or logical force. But for plausibility, for shrewdness, for
power of producing just the turn of thought that the
occasion required, for touching it with vigor and
driving it home, his speeches and his written statements are often remarkable.

As with other forms of self-analysis, I have watched
curiously to see how far Butler himself reflected upon
this terrible power of speech, both for good and for
evil, to speaker and to hearers. His friends saw it
clearly enough: "Speeches of public men are the as-
sassins they bear about with them," warns one.[66] But
I do not find him dissecting it with scientific lucidity.
That he well appreciated its practical bearing appears
in his account of his firing the laborers of Lowell to
fury: "My voice rang out as it can do on occasion. . . .
'As God lives and I live, by the living Jehovah! if one
man is driven from his employment by these men because of his vote, I will lead you to make Lowell what
it was twenty-five years ago — a sheep-pasture and
fishing-place; and I will commence by applying the
torch to my own house!' . . . The effect was marvelous.
A yell broke out like the agonized groan of wild
animals when they feel the deadly knife at their
throats. Some cried out, 'Let us do it now,' and applause broke out all over the hall." [67]

Such things force upon us the significance of words in a democracy, and what they can do, and what they can do for a man like Butler. Words with something behind them make the man who prevails. But even with little behind them, their insinuating dominance is far too overwhelming. One thinks of the rare cases of men like Cleveland who come to the top with practically no words whatever, simply with the driving energy of character. Again, one compares even more directly two such men as Butler and Lincoln. Undeniably there were marked resemblances between them. Both came from the people, both understood the people, both appealed to the people with singular effect and aptitude. Both knew the value of humor and resorted to it with constant freshness and efficacy and with a homely shrewdness approaching, when not reaching, the coarse. Both had the gift of speech in a high degree. The enormous difference, in endowment and in achievement, can only be summed up in the indefinable, but far-reaching, term, character, which we applied to Cleveland. Words without character go far, terribly, dangerously far, in popular government. What words with character will do the career of Lincoln shows. Hitherto the frothing, foaming, restless ocean of popular government has thrown up fifty men of the type of Butler for one of the type of

Lincoln. Those who, with Lincoln, believe in the future of democracy, can only hope that with time it will produce more Lincolns and fewer Butlers.

THE END

NOTES

NOTES

THE notes to each chapter are preceded by a list of the most important works referred to, with the abbreviations used.

II. BENEDICT ARNOLD

Arnold, Isaac N., *The Life of Benedict Arnold, His Patriotism and His Treason*.   Arnold

1. Joshua Hett Smith, *An Authentic Narrative of the Causes Which Led to the Death of Major André*, p. 292.
2. Washington, *Writings* (edition Ford), vol. v, p. 490.
3. Arnold, p. 66.
4. Arnold, p. 48.
5. Jared Sparks, *The Life and Treason of Benedict Arnold*, pp. 5, 6.
6. William Abbatt, *The Crisis of the Revolution*, p. 81.
7. Jared Sparks, *The Life and Treason of Benedict Arnold*, p. 10.
8. Maxwell to Livingston, October 20, 1876, Force, *Archives*. Series V, vol. II, p. 1143.
9. A. T. Mahan, *The Major Operations of the Navies in the War of American Independence*, p. 25.
10. *Ibid.*
11. James Wilkinson, *Memoirs of My Own Times*, vol. I, p. 273.
12. Quoted in Stevens, article on "Benedict Arnold and His Apologist," in *Magazine of American History*, vol. IV, p. 181.
13. *Magazine of American History*, vol. III, p. 83.
14. Arnold, p. 35.
15. Samuel Downing, in Arnold, p. 29.
16. Mrs. Arnold to Arnold, August 13, 1753, quoted by P. L. Ford, in the *Cosmopolitan*, April, 1900, vol. XXVIII, p. 694.
17. Letter of November 27, 1775, in *Maine Historical Society Collections*, vol. I, p. 495.
18. Article by P. L. Ford, in *Cosmopolitan*, vol. XXVIII, p. 695, April, 1900.
19. To Schuyler, in Arnold, p. 241.

NOTES

20. Joshua Hett Smith, *Narrative of the Death of André*, p. 296.
21. Sydney George Fisher, *The Struggle for American Independence*, vol. II, p. 303.
22. Arnold, p. 217.
23. John Fiske, *The American Revolution*, vol. II, p. 207.
24. To Gates, September 7, 1776, Force, *Archives*, Series V, vol. II, p. 224.
25. To Mrs. Arnold, Arnold, p. 234.
26. Manuscript in library of Massachusetts Historical Society, first printed in *My Story: Being the Memoirs of Benedict Arnold*, by F. J. Stimson; p. 333.
27. S. Weir Mitchell, *Hugh Wynne* (edition in one volume), p. 426.
28. Mrs. Ann Willing Morris, in *Life of Margaret Shippen*, by Lewis Bird Walker, in *Pennsylvania Magazine of History and Biography*, vol. xxv, p. 40.
29. Arnold, p. 23.
30. John Codman 2d, *Arnold's Expedition to Quebec*, p. 19.
31. Washington to Reed, in *Life and Correspondence of Joseph Reed*, by William B. Reed, vol. II, p. 55.
32. A. T. Mahan, *The Major Operations of the Navies in the War of American Independence*, p. 27.
33. Thomas Wentworth Higginson, *Margaret Fuller Ossoli*, p. 289.
34. In *My Story*, by F. J. Stimson, p. 334.
35. *Magazine of American History*, vol. IV, p. 191, March, 1880.
36. To Gates, in Arnold, p. 149.
37. To Gates, September 28, 1776, Force, *Archives*, Series V, vol. II, p. 592.
38. September 25, 1780, in Arnold, p. 299.
39. P. L. Ford, in *Cosmopolitan*, vol. xxvIII, p. 702, April, 1900.
40. Joshua Hett Smith, *Narrative of the Death of André*, p. 296.
41. To Joseph Reed, May 28, 1780, in Arnold, p. 273.
42. J. Parton, *The Life and Times of Aaron Burr* (edition, 1858), p. 126.
43. Jesse Rose to Jonathan Trumbull, September 30, 1780, *Trumbull Papers*, part IV, p. 146.
44. Arnold, 363.
45. Joshua Hett Smith, *Narrative of the Death of André*, p. 22.

46. Arnold, p. 129.

47. February 8, 1779, Arnold, p. 230.

48. George Canning Hill, *Benedict Arnold*, p. 216.

49. October 7, 1780, P. L. Ford, in *Cosmopolitan*, vol. xxviii, p. 697, April, 1900.

50. To Mrs. Greene, September 28, 1780, in Greene's *Life of Greene*, vol. ii, p. 232.

51. September 27, 1780, *Magazine of American History*, vol. iv, p. 190, March, 1880.

52. Albert Bushnell Hart, *The Varick Court of Inquiry*, p. 162.

53. To Laurens, October 13, 1780, *Works* (Ford), vol. viii, p. 494.

54. *Ibid.*

55. Arnold, p. 347.

56. To father, July 6, 1792, *Pennsylvania Magazine of History and Biography*, vol. xxv, p. 462.

57. To E. Burd, August 15, 1801, *Pennsylvania Magazine*, vol. xxv, p. 474.

58. Arnold, p. 400.

59. *Pennsylvania Magazine*, vol. xxv, p. 474.

60. To Miss Schuyler, September 25, 1780, *Works* (Lodge), vol. viii, p. 17.

61. To father, March 6, 1786, *Pennsylvania Magazine*, vol. xxv, p. 167.

62. To father, July 6, 1792, *ibid.*, p. 171.

63. *Ibid.*, p. 170.

64. Arnold, p. 397.

65. Arnold, p. 395.

66. Prince de Talleyrand, *Memoirs*, translated by R. L. de Beaufort, vol. i, p. 174.

67. Henry C. Van Schaack, *The Life of Peter Van Schaack*, vol. ii, p. 147.

68. See Sargent's *André*, p. 421, and Fiske's *American Revolution*, vol. ii, p. 234.

III. THOMAS PAINE

Conway, Moncure Daniel, *The Life of Thomas Paine*, two volumes.   Conway.

Paine, Thomas, *The Writings of Thomas Paine, collected and edited by Moncure Daniel Conway*, four volumes. (The edition of Wheeler, ten volumes, seems to add little to Conway.) *Writings.*

1. Ellery Sedgwick, *Thomas Paine*, p. 61.
2. *Ibid.*, p. 93.
3. *Writings*, vol. II, p. 328.
4. *Writings*, vol. II, p. 402.
5. *Writings*, vol. I, p. 375.
6. *Writings*, vol. I, p. 181.
7. *Writings*, vol. II, p. 77.
8. *Writings*, vol. I, p. 99.
9. *Writings*, vol. I, p. 174.
10. Conway, vol. I, p. 69.
11. Quoted by Elbert Hubbard, in *Life and Writings of Thomas Paine*, edited by Daniel Edwin Wheeler, 10 volumes; vol. I, p. 131.
12. George Otto Trevelyan, *The American Revolution*, part II, vol. I, p. 150.
13. Conway, vol. I, p. 161.
14. To Le Veillard, April 15, 1787, *Works* (edition, Smyth), vol. IX, p. 562.
15. To J. Reed, January 31, 1776, *Works* (edition, Ford), vol. III, p. 396.
16. To J. Reed, April 1, 1776, *Works* (Ford) vol. IV, p. 4.
17. Conway, vol. I, p. 86.
18. Paine himself to Yorke, in Henry Redhead Yorke, *France in Eighteen Hundred and Two* (edition, 1906), p. 240.
19. To Franklin, March 31, 1787, Conway, vol. I, p. 223.
20. William Cobbett, *The Life of Thomas Paine*, by Peter Porcupine, p. 58.
21. *Ibid.*, p. 60.
22. *Works*, vol. III, p. 130.
23. *Works*, vol. III, p. 217.
24. *Works*, vol. III, p. 341.
25. Conway, vol. I, p. 52.

26. Conway, vol. I, p. 44.

27. *Works*, vol. II, p. 493.

28. *Works*, vol. II, p. 491.

29. *Works*, vol. I, p. 63.

30. Conway, vol. II, p. 370.

31. *Works*, vol. IV, p. 22.

32. *Works*, vol. IV, p. 359.

33. Conway, vol. II, p. 195.

34. *Works*, vol. IV, p. 65.

35. *Works*, vol. IV, p. 76.

36. *Works*, vol. IV, p. 254.

37. *Works*, vol. I, p. 176.

38. Conway, vol. II, p. 370.

39. Jefferson's *Works* (Memorial edition, 1903), vol. XVIII, p. 414.

40. *Ibid.*, vol. X, p. 299.

41. *Works*, vol. II, p. 232.

42. *Works*, vol. IV, p. 433.

43. Conway, vol. I, p. 35.

44. Conway, vol. I, p. 34.

45. Conway, vol. I, p. 248.

46. Thomas Clio Rickman, *The Life of Thomas Paine*, p. 101.

47. *Ibid.*, p. xv.

48. Conway, vol. II, p. 474.

49. *Works*, vol. I, p. 26.

50. W. T. Sherwin, *Memoir of the Life of Thomas Paine*, p. 201.

51. Conway, in *Works*, vol. III, p. xv.

52. Conway, vol. I, p. 148.

53. Note in *Account of Arnold's Campaign against Quebec*, by J. Henry, p. 126.

54. Theodore Roosevelt, *Gouverneur Morris*, p. 289.

55. Conway, vol. II, p. 456.

56. Howell's *State Trials*, vol. XXII, p. 402.

57. *Works*, vol. II, p. 256.

58. Conway, vol. II, p. 395.

59. Jefferson to Paine, September 6, 1807, Jefferson, *Works* (Memorial edition, 1903), vol. XI, p. 362.

60. *Works*, vol. II, p. 462.

61. *Works*, vol. I, p. 55.
62. *Works*, vol. I, p. 185.
63. Thomas Clio Rickman, *The Life of Thomas Paine*, p. 65.
64. Massachusetts Historical Society, *Proceedings*, Series **II**, vol xx, p. 279.
65. James Cheetham, *The Life of Thomas Paine*, p. 280.
66. Conway, vol. I, p. 214.
67. *Works*, vol. I, p. 196.
68. Conway, vol. I, p. 249.
69. *Works*, vol. III, p. 398.
70. *Works*, vol. II, p. 463.
71. Conway, vol. II, p. 367.
72. *Works*, vol. IV, p. 88.
73. *Works*, vol. IV, p. 151.
74. Conway, vol. I, p. 326.
75. *Works*, vol. II, p. 204.
76. *Works*, vol. II, pp. 121, 122.
77. P. W. Clayden, *The Early Life of Samuel Rogers*, p. 246.

IV. AARON BURR

Burr, Aaron, *The Private Journal of*, edited by William K. Bixby, two volumes. Bixby.

Burr, Aaron, *The Private Journal of*, edited by Matthew L. Davis, two volumes. *Journal* (Davis).

Davis, Matthew L., *Memoirs of Aaron Burr*, two volumes. *Memoirs*.

Parton, J., *The Life and Times of Aaron Burr* (edition, 1858). Parton.

1. John Quincy Adams, *Memoirs*, vol. IX, p. 429.
2. Charles Burr Todd, *Life of Colonel Aaron Burr*, p. 127.
3. *Portraits Contemporains*, vol. v, p. 464.
4. *Memoirs*, vol. II, p. 243.
5. Parton, p. 658.
6. *Journal* (Davis), vol. II, p. 117.
7. Frederick Scott Oliver, *Alexander Hamilton*, p. 419.
8. Henry Cabot Lodge, *Alexander Hamilton*, p. 248.

NOTES

9. Frederick Scott Oliver, *Alexander Hamilton*, p. 419.
10. Bixby, vol. I, p. 337.
11. William H. Safford, *The Blennerhassett Papers*, p. 469.
12. *Memoirs*, vol. I, p. 295.
13. Bixby, vol. II, p. 147.
14. *The Diary of Samuel Pepys* (edition, Wheatley), vol. IV, p. 221.
15. *Memoirs*, vol. II, p. 371.
16. Parton, p. 622.
17. Parton, p. 682.
18. Parton, p. 685.
19. Parton, p. 623.
20. *Memoirs*, vol. II, p. 14.
21. Charles Burr Todd, *Life of Colonel Aaron Burr*, p. 89.
22. Parton, p. 283.
23. Burr to Jeremy Bentham, January 23, 1809, *Journal* (Davis), vol. I, p. 169.
24. Hamilton's statement as to duel, printed in *Memoirs*, vol. II, p. 319.
25. Frederick Scott Oliver, *Alexander Hamilton*, p. 420.
26. Parton, p. 673.
27. *Annals of Congress*, 1804–05, p. 71.
28. John Quincy Adams, *Memoirs*, vol. I, p. 366.
29. *History of the United States*, vol. III, chapters X–XIV.
30. Walter Flavius McCaleb, *The Aaron Burr Conspiracy*.
31. Henry Cabot Lodge, *Alexander Hamilton*, p. 247.
32. *Journal* (Davis), vol. I, p. 115.
33. Bixby, vol. II, p. 462.
34. Bixby, vol. II, p. 114.
35. Charles Burr Todd, *Life of Colonel Aaron Burr*, p. 133.
36. Bixby, vol. II, p. 319.
37. Bixby, vol. II, p. 244.
38. Bixby, vol. I, p. 146.
39. Bixby, vol. I, p. 209.
40. *Journal* (Davis), vol. I, p. 234.
41. *Memoirs*, vol. I, p 45.
42. Parton, p. 626.
43. Parton, p. 675.

44. Parton, p. 626.
45. Bixby, vol. II, p. 347.
46. Bixby, vol. II, p. 350.
47. Bixby, vol. I, p. 357.
48. Bixby, vol. II, p. 9.
49. Edward Channing, *A History of the United States*, vol. IV, p. 236.
50. Bixby, vol. II, p. 9.
51. *Journal* (Davis), vol. I, p. 285.
52. William H. Safford, *The Blennerhassett Papers*, p. 259.
53. Bixby, vol. II, p. 471.
54. Parton, p. 675.
55. Bixby, vol. II, p. 192.
56. Charles Burr Todd, *Life of Colonel Aaron Burr*, p. 129.
57. Bixby, vol. II, p. 25.
58. Parton, p. 615.
59. James Shirley, *Works* (edition, Dyce), vol. I, p. 350.

V. JOHN RANDOLPH OF ROANOKE

Adams, Henry, *John Randolph*.   **Adams.**

Bouldin, Powhatan, *Home Reminiscences of John Randolph of Roanoke*.   **Bouldin.**

Bruce, William Cabell, *John Randolph of Roanoke*, two volumes.   **Bruce.**

Garland, Hugh A., *The Life of John Randolph of Roanoke*, two volumes.   **Garland.**

Randolph, John, *Letters to a Young Relative*.   *Letters.*

1. Bouldin, p. 1.
2. Edward Channing, *A History of the United States*, vol. IV, p. 287.
3. Henry Adams, *History of the United States of America*, vol. III, p. 157.
4. Bouldin, p. 158.
5. Bruce, vol. I, p. 633.
6. Henry Adams, *The Life of Albert Gallatin*, p. 332.
7. Speech of April 7, 1806, *Annals of Congress*, 1805–06, p. 984.

NOTES

8. Josiah Quincy, *Figures of the Past*, p. 227.

9. Garland, vol. I, p. 176.

10. Garland, vol. II, p. 91.

11. Garland, vol. II, pp. 93, 94.

12. Lemuel Sawyer, *Biography of John Randolph of Roanoke*, p. 111.

13. Bruce, vol. II, p. 6.

14. Bouldin, p. 264.

15. Garland, vol. II, p. 217.

16. Garland, vol. I, p. 21.

17. Bruce, vol. I, p. 175.

18. Henry Adams, *History of the United States of America*, vol. III, p. 164, from *Annals of Congress*.

19. Adams, p. 25.

20. Adams, p. 271, Garland, vol. II, p. 149.

21. Garland, vol. II, p. 150.

22. Garland, vol. II, p. 101.

23. Adams, p. 288.

24. Garland, vol. II, p. 239; Bruce, vol. II, p. 633.

25. Garland, vol. II, p. 102.

26. Garland, vol. II, p. 103.

27. John Bach McMaster, *A History of the People of the United States*, vol. II, p. 457.

28. Garland, vol. II, p. 238.

29. Adams, p. 19.

30. Bruce, vol. I, p. 283, from Garland, vol. II, p. 346.

31. Garland, vol. II, p. 154.

32. Bouldin, p. 124.

33. Manasseh Cutler to Captain F. Poole, February 13, 1804, in *Life, Journals, and Correspondence of Rev. Manasseh Cutler*, vol. II, p. 162. The name is printed *Ashton* in the Life of Cutler, but from Bruce, vol. I, pp. 362, 363, it is evident that *Alston* is meant.

34. Garland, vol. I, p. 159.

35. Daniel Webster, *Private Correspondence*, vol. I, p. 259.

36. *Ibid.*, p. 258.

37. Garland, vol. II, p. 254.

38. Adams, p. 287.

39. Garland, vol. I, p. 77.

40. Adams, p. 24.

41. Garland, vol. II, p. 327.

42. Garland, vol. II, p. 42.

43. Garland, vol. I, p. 18.

44. Garland, vol. II, p. 101.

45. Garland, vol. II, p. 44.

46. Bouldin, p. 86.

47. Garland, vol. II, p. 96.

48. Bouldin, p. 80.

49. Lemuel Sawyer, *Biography of John Randolph of Roanoke*, p. 112.

50. George Ticknor, *Life, Letters, and Journals*, vol. I, p. 16.

51. Bruce, vol. I, p. 639.

52. *The Letters of Washington Irving to Henry Brevoort*, vol. II, p. 175.

53. Pierre M. Irving, *The Life and Letters of Washington Irving*, vol. II, p. 441.

54. Josiah Quincy, *Figures of the Past*, p. 216.

55. Garland, vol. I, p. 261.

56. *Letters*, p. 207.

57. *Letters*, p. 156.

58. Garland, vol. I, p. 167.

59. Bouldin, p. 292.

60. Bruce, vol. II, p. 319.

61. Garland, vol. I, p. 184.

62. *Ibid.*

63. Bruce, vol. II, p. 326.

64. Bruce, vol. I, p. 101.

65. Bruce, vol. II, p. 273.

66. Bruce, vol. II, pp. 524–537.

67. *Letters*, p. 203.

68. Garland, vol. II, p. 258.

69. Garland, vol. I, p. 72.

70. Garland, vol. I, p. 71.

71. Garland, vol. II, p. 367.

72. Garland, vol. I, p. 27.

73. Garland, vol. II, p. 91.

74. Garland, vol. II, p. 68.

75. Garland, vol. II, p. 107.
76. Garland, vol. II, p. 111.
77. Garland, vol. II, p. 293.
78. Garland, vol. II, p. 89.
79. Garland, vol. II, p. 90.
80. Garland, vol. II, p. 294.
81. Garland, vol. II, p. 80.
82. Garland, vol. II, p. 68.
83. Garland, vol. II, p. 288.
84. *Letters*, p. 106.
85. Garland, vol. II, p. 147.

VI. JOHN BROWN

Sanborn, F. B., *Life and Letters of John Brown.*   Sanborn.
Villard, Oswald Garrison, *John Brown.*   Villard.
Wilson, Hill Peebles, *John Brown, Soldier of Fortune.*   Wilson.

1. Letter of N. Eggleston, October, 1883, in Sara T. D. Robinson, *Kansas* (edition, 1899), p. 414.
2. Wilson, p. 44.
3. *The Life and Times of Frederick Douglass, Written by Himself* (edition, 1883), p. 337.
4. F. B. Sanborn, *Recollections of Seventy Years*, vol. I, p. 152.
5. Printed in Wilson, Appendix III.
6. Richard D. Webb, *The Life and Letters of Captain John Brown*, p. 106.
7. Villard, p. 424.
8. To Higginson, May 14, 1858, Boston Public Library MS.
9. James Redpath, *The Public Life of Capt. John Brown*, p. 395
10. Villard, p. 555.
11. Sanborn, p. 140.
12. Sanborn, p. 122.
13. To the Rev. John Newton, September 9, 1781.
14. William M. Hunt's *Talks on Art*, Series II, p. 66.
15. *The Life and Times of Frederick Douglass*, p. 338.
16. *Ibid.*
17. *Ibid.*

NOTES

18. Sanborn, p. 117.
19. Mrs. Marcus Spring, in Richard D. Webb, *The Life and Letters of Captain John Brown*, p. 297.
20. Sanborn, p. 24.
21. Sanborn, p. 92.
22. Villard, p. 36.
23. Dr. Edward Emerson, in *Journals of Ralph Waldo Emerson*, vol. IX, p. 83.
24. Wilson, p. 131.
25. *The Life and Times of Frederick Douglass*, p. 338.
26. Villard, p. 320.
27. Vorrede zum ersten Bande der Campe'schen Ausgabe des Salons.
28. Sanborn, p. 609.
29. Villard, p. 507.
30. Villard, p. 323.
31. Villard, p. 323.
32. Villard, p. 5.
33. Sanborn, p. 444.
34. Wilson, p. 130.
35. Sanborn, p. 33.
36. Villard, p. 20.
37. Sanborn, p. 600.
38. Villard, p. 200.
39. James Redpath, *The Public Life of Capt. John Brown*, p. 226.
40. Villard, p. 310.
41. Villard, p. 552.
42. Sanborn, p. 259.
43. Villard, p. 496.
44. Sanborn, p. 593.
45. James Redpath, *The Public Life of Capt. John Brown*, p. 377.
46. Villard, p. 510.
47. Letter of Douglass, in F. B. Sanborn, *Recollections of Seventy Years*, vol. I, p. 249.
48. Sanborn, p. 446.
49. Villard, p. 496.
50. Henry David Thoreau, *Journal*, vol. XII, p. 438.

NOTES

VII. PHINEAS TAYLOR BARNUM

Barnum, P. T., *The Life of, Written by Himself*, 1855. *Life*, 1855.
Barnum, P. T., *Struggles and Triumphs; or, Forty Years' Recollections*, 1875.   *Life*, 1875.
Barnum, P. T., *Struggles and Triumphs; or, Forty Years' Recollections*, 1880.   *Life*, 1880.

1. *Life*, 1855, p. 274.
2. Joel Benton, in *Century*, vol. LXIV, p. 589.
3. *Life*, 1875, p. 135.
4. P. T. Barnum, *The Humbugs of the World*, p. 28.
5. Nancy Barnum, *The Last Chapter*, p. 14.
6. P. T. Barnum, *The Humbugs of the World*, p. 53.
7. *Life*, 1875, p. 689.
8. *Life*, 1875, p. 767.
9. *Life*, 1875, p. 726.
10. *Life*, 1855, p. 13.
11. *Life*, 1875, p. 271.
12. *Life*, 1855, p. 390.
13. Joel Benton, in *Century*, vol. LXIV, p. 587.
14. *Life*, 1855, p. 107.
15. *Life*, 1855, p. 99.
16. *Life*, 1875, preface.
17. Mr. M. R. Werner, letter to the author.
18. New York *Tribune*, April 8, 1891.
19. *Life*, 1855, p. 129.
20. *Life*, 1855, p. 858.
21. *Life*, 1875, p. 139.
22. P. T. Barnum, *The Humbugs of the World*, p. 66.
23. *Life*, 1875, p. 494.
24. Joel Benton, in *Century*, vol. LXIV, p. 587.
25. *Life*, 1875, p. 373.
26. *Life*, 1875, p. 81.
27. *Life*, 1855, p. 243.
28. *Life*, 1875, p. 272.
29. *Life*, 1875, p. 203.
30. *Life*, 1875, p. 493.

31. *Life*, 1875, p. 608.
32. *Life*, 1855, p. 225.
33. *Life*, 1875, p. 149.
34. *Life*, 1875, p. 548.
35. P. T. Barnum, *Why I am a Universalist*, p. 9.
36. *Life*, 1875, p. 63.
37. *Life*, 1875, p. 151.
38. Nancy Barnum, *The Last Chapter*, p. 3.
39. George Conklin, *The Ways of the Circus*, p. 253.
40. P. T. Barnum, *The Humbugs of the World*, p. 220.
41. *Life*, 1875, p. 72.
42. *Life*, 1880, p. 314.
43. *Life*, 1875, p. 201.
44. Joel Benton, in *Century*, vol. LXIV, p. 581.
45. *Life*, 1855, p. 120.
46. *Life*, 1875, p. 345.
47. *Life*, 1875, p. 229.
48. *Life*, 1855, p. 94.
49. *Life*, 1855, p. 171.
50. *Life*, 1875, p. 856.
51. *Life*, 1855, p. 399.
52. London *World*, of March, 1877, in *Life*, 1880, p. 318 (tenses changed).
53. Joel Benton, in *Century*, vol. LXIV, p. 583.
54. P. T. Barnum, *Why I am a Universalist*, p. 9.

VIII. BENJAMIN FRANKLIN BUTLER

Butler, Benjamin F., *Butler's Book, Autobiography and Personal Reminiscences.*   *Butler's Book.*

Butler, Benjamin F., *Private and Official Correspondence of, during the Period of the Civil War*, five volumes.   *Correspondence.*

1. To Edward L. Pierce, August 15, 1861, *Correspondence*, vol. I, p. 216.
2. *Argument before the Tewksbury Investigation Committee*, p. 12.
3. William E. Chandler, *Address before the Grafton and Coös Bar Association*, p. 14.

NOTES

4. George F. Hoar, *Autobiography of Seventy Years*, vol. I, p. 330.
5. John Fiske, *The Mississippi Valley in the Civil War*, p. 131.
6. To Grant, July 3, 1864, *Correspondence*, vol. IV, p. 458.
7. To Grant, July 2, 1864, *Official Records*, vol. 81, p. 595.
8. To Halleck, May 24, 1864, *Correspondence*, vol. IV, p. 258.
9. To Porter, *Official Records*, vol. 99, p. 69.
10. William Preston Johnston, *The Life of Gen. Albert Sidney Johnston*, p. 736.
11. James Ford Rhodes, *A History of the United States*, vol. VI, p. 389.
12. *U.S. Reports (Supreme Court)*, vol. 144, p. 65.
13. James Ford Rhodes, *A History of the United States*, vol. V, p. 312.
14. To Chase, September 9, 1862, *Correspondence*, vol. II, p. 271.
15. *Correspondence*, vol. II, p. 499.
16. *Correspondence*, vol. I, p. 203.
17. June 21, 1864, *Correspondence*, vol. IV, p. 430.
18. To Mrs. Heard, November 28, 1862, *Correspondence*, vol. II, p. 503.
19. *Correspondence*, vol. V, p. 547.
20. James Parton, *General Butler in New Orleans*, p. 183.
21. *Correspondence*, vol. I, p. 307.
22. *Correspondence*, vol. III, p. 130.
23. *Correspondence*, vol. III, p. 29.
24. George S. Merriam, *The Life and Times of Samuel Bowles*, vol. II, p. 435.
25. *Butler's Book*, p. 550.
26. *Harper's Magazine*, December, 1914, p. 100.
27. J. R. Young, *Around the World with General Grant*, vol. II, p. 304.
28. James Ford Rhodes, *A History of the United States*, vol. VII, p. 24, and J. H. Wilson, *Life of Charles A. Dana*, p. 336.
29. Wilson, *Dana*, p. 483.
30. *Correspondence*, vol. II, p. 44.
31. Letter to author.
32. To Butler, June 6, 1864, *Correspondence*, vol. IV, p. 318.
33. *Correspondence*, vol. II, p. 218.
34. *Correspondence*, vol. I, p. 208.

NOTES

35. *Correspondence*, vol. I, p. 204.
36. *Correspondence*, vol. IV, p. 375.
37. *Correspondence*, vol. IV, p. 342.
38. *Correspondence*, vol. II, p. 201.
39. *Trial of Andrew Johnson*, vol. I, p. 104.
40. Speech in Music Hall, Boston, October 10, 1883, in Springfield *Republican*, October 12, 1883.
41. Maunsell B. Field, *Memories of Many Men*, p. 287.
42. *Correspondence*, vol. II, p. 215.
43. *Argument before the Tewksbury Investigation Committee*, p. 35.
44. *Correspondence*, vol. V, p. 72.
45. *Butler's Book*, p. 871.
46. *Argument before the Tewksbury Investigation Committee*, p. 12.
47. Moorfield Storey, *The Record of Benjamin F. Butler*, p. 6.
48. Morris Schaff, *Jefferson Davis, His Life and Personality*, p. 213.
49. *Argument before the Tewksbury Investigation Committee*, p. 42.
50. To Butler, August 8, 1862, *Correspondence*, vol. II, p. 165.
51. To Lincoln, November 29, 1862, *Correspondence*, vol. II, p. 514.
52. September 9, 1862, *Correspondence*, vol. II, p. 272.
53. Carl Schurz, *Reminiscences*, vol. II, p. 225.
54. *Butler's Book*, p. 221.
55. To Birney, July 27, 1864, *Correspondence*, vol. IV, p. 549.
56. Speech in Music Hall, Boston, October 10, 1883, in Springfield *Republican*, October 12, 1883.
57. *Butler's Book*, p. 989, 1031.
58. Speech of September 1, 1873, in Springfield *Republican*, September 2, 1873.
59. *Butler's Book*, p. 1036.
60. *Correspondence*, vol. V, p. 476.
61. *Butler's Book*, p. 416.
62. *Butler's Book*, p. 860.
63. *Butler's Book*, p. 871.
64. *Butler's Book*, p. 812.
65. To Mrs. Butler, September 15, 1864, *Correspondence*, vol. V, p. 136.
66. *Correspondence*, vol. III, p. 79.
67. *Butler's Book*, p. 104.